Middle School Healthy Hearts in the Zone

A Heart Rate Monitoring Program for Lifelong Fitness

Deve Swaim and Sally Edwards

Heart Zone Education

Human Kinetics

Library of Congress Cataloging-in-Publication Data

Swaim, Deve, 1951-
  Middle school healthy hearts in the zone: a heart rate monitoring program for lifelong fitness / by Deve Swaim and Sally Edwards.
      p. cm.
  Includes bibliographical references (p.) and index.
  ISBN 0-7360-4176-1
    1. Exercise for children. 2. Heart rate monitoring. 3. Middle school students--Health and hygiene. 4. Cardiovascular fitness. I. Edwards, Sally 1947- II. Title.

  RJ133 .S93 2002
  613.7'043--dc21

                                        2001039551

ISBN: 0-7360-4176-1

Acquisitions Editor: Scott Wikgren; **Developmental Editor:** Renee T. Thomas; **Assistant Editor:** Amanda S. Ewing; **Copyeditor:** Jennifer M. Thompson; **Proofreader:** Anne Meyer Byler; **Indexer:** Daniel Connolly; **Permission Manager:** Dalene Reeder; **Graphic Designer:** Stuart Cartwright; **Graphic Artist:** Denise Lowry; **Cover Designer:** Stuart Cartwright; **Art Managers:** Craig Newsom and Carl Johnson; **Illustrator:** Craig Newsom; **Printer:** Versa Press

Printed in the United States of America   10   9   8   7   6   5   4   3   2   1

Human Kinetics
Web site: www.humankinetics.com

United States: Human Kinetics, P.O. Box 5076, Champaign, IL 61825-5076
800-747-4457
e-mail: humank@hkusa.com

Canada: Human Kinetics, 475 Devonshire Road Unit 100, Windsor, ON N8Y 2L5
800-465-7301 (in Canada only)
e-mail: orders@hkcanada.com

Europe: Human Kinetics, Units C2/C3 Wira Business Park, West Park Ring Road, Leeds LS16 6EB, United Kingdom
+44 (0) 113 278 1708
e-mail: hk@hkeurope.com

Australia: Human Kinetics, 57A Price Avenue, Lower Mitcham, South Australia 5062
08 8277 1555
e-mail: liahka@senet.com.au

New Zealand: Human Kinetics, P.O. Box 105-231, Auckland Central
09-523-3462
e-mail: hkp@ihug.co.nz

CONTENTS

PREFACE:
WELCOME TO HEART ZONE TRAINING

The program described in this book offers the tools, the instructions, the data, and the support for teaching students to design and reach their personal fitness goals. The program is based on the principles of "Heart Zone Training," a comprehensive wellness program that looks at the wellness continuum from three views: health, fitness, and performance. As you teach Heart Zone Training, you and your students will select which wellness area to work in on any given day:

- To improve *health*, by lowering their blood pressure and cholesterol levels and seeing weight loss or stability
- To improve *fitness*, as measured by improved cardiovascular capacity
- To improve athletic *performance*, by raising their anaerobic threshold as close as possible to their maximum heart rate

 The losses from the war with cardiovascular disease are greater in a single year than in all of the wars America has ever fought. It is the single largest cause of death of Americans.

This has been and continues to be a work in progress. As we learn more from you, we revise and add to the curriculum. Please give us your feedback so we may all continue to learn. You can contact us on the Internet at **www.Heartzones.com**.

ACKNOWLEDGMENTS

This project was several years in the making and was bettered by the handling of many people along the way. Special thanks to the following people:

Cheryl Miller, Judson Middle School, Salem, Oregon

Debra C. Harris, West Linn High School, West Linn, Oregon

Judy Stansbury, Del Oro High School, Loomis, California

Mike Fischer, Manhattan Elementary School, Montana

Glenn Warry, Heart Zones Australia, Brisbane, Australia

Rob Kerr, Arcade Middle School, Sacramento, California

Randy Quinto, Juneau, Alaska

Pietro Michelucci, Heartware, Sacramento, California

Luana Hill, Hill Publishing, Canby, Oregon

Mary Burroughs, Burroughs Publication and Design, Sacramento, California

Sally Reed, Heart Zones Cycling, Seattle, Washington

Chet Bradley, Department of Public Instruction, Wisconsin

Carl Nickerson, Comprehensive Health Education Foundation, Washington

Randy Cottrell, University of Cincinnati, Ohio

Jeanie White, McNary High School, Salem, Oregon

Dawn Graf-Haight, Linfield College, Oregon

Chris Wentworth, Health & Fitness Medical, Mill Valley, California

We are especially thankful to the team at Human Kinetics for their support and contributions toward making this goal succeed. Thank you to Scott Wikgren for seeing the possibilities here and inviting us into the HK family.

HOW TO USE THIS BOOK

This is the first simple-to-use book to help teachers effectively use heart rate monitors in health and physical education programs. This program uses the heart muscles and an organized system, Heart Zone Training, to guide students through successful fitness development. It is structured with clear explanations of the material, lessons, skills, and activities.

Seven Foundational Principles of Heart Rate Monitoring Programs

1. Heart Rate Monitor Programs for Health and Physical Education (HRMP) is revolutionary and new. It develops strategies for adapting technological equipment for classroom use. This leading-edge approach to learning will revitalize the curriculum.

2. HRMP is integrative. It integrates easily with mathematics, biological science, computer science, physical education, and creative writing.

3. HRMP is relevant. It provides immediate, personal, and individualized feedback.

4. HRMP provides a link with technology. With technology we can better manage change as progress occurs.

5. HRMP guides personal growth. It motivates goal setting.

6. HRMP is a system for managing your wellness. It demonstrates the interdependence of emotional, mental, and physical health.

7. HRMP teaches health management. It provides quantifiable biofeedback for assessing health levels.

Goals and Standards of Heart Zone Training Curricula

Heart Zone Training (HZT) is a program designed to allow each student to set and reach optimal wellness goals. The goals and standards of the HZT curricula are

- to become competent in using a heart rate monitor;
- to become competent in monitoring, assessing, and managing cardiac data;
- to motivate health maintenance and promote wellness;
- to develop decision-making competencies for health and healthy behavior;
- to design a health maintenance and improvement plan based on the knowledge gained from using a heart rate monitor; and
- to design "smart" goals based on individual stages of development and current fitness level.

Rationale for Using Heart Rate Monitors

Basic to our health education is an understanding of the relationship between behavior and health as well as a means for assessing that relationship. As educators and learners we must develop methods for setting realistic, achievable goals—based on proven methods—specific to our bodies and interests. These goals need to be assessed by a measurement tool designed to show the individual's continuous progress toward attainment.

The wellness education of our children is not a simple task, and to date it is not one we have done well. We have failed, and the reason is only just now becoming clear. Our failure was rooted in one basic premise: What works for one child works for all. In fact, it didn't work, and the net effect is what we see today: kids becoming more sedentary and less fit with little or no hope that they can ever get fit.

We know a great deal more about the impact of today's lifestyle on tomorrow's health than we did a generation ago, yet we remain a nation at risk. The 1996 Surgeon General's Report on Physical Activity and Health tells us that 13.5 million Americans have coronary heart disease, 1.5 million suffer heart attacks every year, and more then 60 million (a third of the population) are overweight. The report further indicates that of adolescents ages 12 to 21, nearly half are not vigorously active on a regular basis.

Students' wellness levels differ, and performance can be affected by many factors. With HZT each student can assess his own needs, make adjustments to attain goals, and measure improvement. We accomplish this with new technological health hardware that monitors the heart's response—a heart rate monitor.

Heart Zone Training is a method for matching heart zones, a range of heartbeats, to a fitness goal. Exercise in different heart zones achieves different results, thereby allowing individualized programs for each student.

Through constant feedback, the student learns to improve her performance and maximize her time in class. There is no other program of its kind that can accomplish this. In the past, outcomes were judged on a "norm" or "perceived performance" standard. With HZT you can devise a program based on biofeedback data unique to each student. How is this done?

Let's look at the "health-literate" student as one who has the skills to maintain a level of optimal health throughout life. With a student's knowledge of and skill for recognizing his body's response to stimuli such as stress, exercise, and diet, he can more accurately determine his best fit with a wellness lifestyle.

Are students interested in knowing how to prevent disease and obesity and how to maintain good health? According to the "Students Speak" survey, a survey of more than five thousand K-12 students in Washington state, 91 percent of the sixth-graders responding were very interested or somewhat interested in how to be healthy. Ninety-six percent of the eighth-graders wanted to know how to be physically fit and 86 percent of the ninth-graders polled wanted to know how to maintain an appropriate weight throughout life. Students are very interested in the health of their bodies.

The American Medical Association for National Health Education Standards states: "It is the growing belief that any future advances made in improving the nation's health will not result from spectacular biomedical breakthroughs. Rather, advances will result from personally initiated actions that are directly influenced by the individual's health-related attitudes, beliefs, and knowledge. School health education can make a valuable contribution in areas such as these and can play an important role in improving the quality of living."

After more then 20 years in education, we are thrilled to be part of the movement to bring HZT into classrooms. This new technology advancement in hardware and training provides the immediate feedback often lacking in current wellness programs and provides a new stimulus for student and teacher alike. Its universal application also will motivate teachers to assess their own wellness and follow the lessons that they are teaching.

Curriculum Format

Our goal is to provide the educator with a supplemental curriculum that will enhance a learner's ability to make responsible decisions regarding a healthy lifestyle. Its purpose is to provide tools to help students take an active role in maintaining and improving their health while augmenting the teacher's current curriculum with the latest technology advances.

Heart technology curricula provide instant cardiac information and feedback. The efficiency of the program assures the teacher's ability to maximize instruction. It also allows the student to make the best use of technology to monitor, assess, and manage her lifestyle and health. This heart technology program's teacher's manual includes

- background information on heart physiology,
- lesson plans for grades five through nine, and
- black-line teaching and student worksheet masters.

This curriculum is organized into five modules that cover applications for teaching students how to use heart rate monitors through applying that learning to designing their personal fitness program.

The program can be taught as a single unit of three to four weeks or in a two-week introductory format with ongoing applications throughout the school year. No matter the approach you use, the modules build on one another.

Each unit begins with a focus for that section and includes a series of lesson plans along with activities and student worksheets. An important component of the program is the gathering and recording of personal heart rate response data.

Glossary of Relevant Terms

aerobic exercise—An exercise program easy enough to keep you from getting out of breath; literally, your muscles are kept "in the presence of oxygen."

alarm—Standard clock alarm feature on monitors.

ambient heart rate—The number of beats per minute your heart contracts when you are awake but in a sedentary and stationary position. Norms range between 60 and 90 beats per minute.

anaerobic exercise—The opposite condition from aerobic; the exercise bout is so strenuous that the muscles are working without sufficient oxygen, called an anaerobic state.

anaerobic threshold—The point at which your body is producing more lactic acid than can be metabolized, also known as the "lactate threshold."

bpm—Beats per minute. This refers to heartbeat.

carbohydrates—Organic compounds that, when broken down, become a main energy source for muscular work.

cardiac—Pertaining to the heart.

delta heart rate—The measure of your heart rate response from a change in body position.

download—The recovery of information stored on the monitor from your workout, either manually or through a computer interface.

fats—Concentrated sources of energy for muscular work. They are compounds containing glycerol and fatty acids and may be saturated or unsaturated.

FIT—The letters stand for frequency, intensity, and time as they relate to a fitness workout. F = Frequency—how often. I = Intensity—the percentage of maximum heart rate in which the workout falls. T = Time—how much time is spent.

heartbeat—A single, complete contraction of the heart.

heart rate—The number of heartbeats per minute.

heart rate functions—The different features that the heart monitor watch provides, such as the ability to display current heart rate.

heart rate memory—A feature of some monitors that store heart rate data for later review by the user.

heart rate or cardiac monitor—An electronic device that measures the electrical activity of the heart and displays it.

heart rate recall—A feature of those monitors that have memory allowing the downloading of the information that is stored in memory.

heart rate reserve (HRR)—The total number of beats (the specific heart rate range) that you have between your resting heart rate and your maximum heart rate. MHRR is the maximum heart rate reserve, and it is sometimes called the "working heart rate."

heart rate watch—An electronic device that combines a time-of-day watch with the features of a heart rate monitor in one unit.

heart zones—A range of heart rates that represents different benefits that occur from exercising or training within their numeric limits.

intensity—The degree of energy, difficulty, or strength, as relates to a workout.

intervals—The duration of a given intensity of training.

limits—The dividing lines of a heart zone; the top of a limit is the ceiling and the bottom of a limit is its floor.

maximum heart rate—The highest number of times your heart can contract in one minute. It can be measured by taking a stress test, using a heart rate monitor, or estimated by using a variety of submaximum assessments.

metabolism—The chemical changes in the body's cells by which energy is provided for vital processes.

mindful recovery—A practiced process for consciously reducing your heart rate.

pulse—The rhythmical throbbing of arteries produced by the regular contractions of the heart, especially as palpated at the wrist or in the neck.

pulse rate—Taken manually, this refers to the measurable rate of the biomechanical blood flow through your arteries.

recall—The playback mode for the recorded data of a heart rate monitor.

record—The storage mode of a heart rate monitor.

recovery heart rate—The number of beats per minute your heart rate drops after cessation of exercise. The higher your fitness level, the faster the drop in your heart rate. A common recovery heart rate measurement is one minute.

resting heart rate—The number of beats your heart contracts in 60 seconds when you first wake up, before you lift your head off the pillow and sit up in bed. You can come close to a resting heart rate if you lie down and are relatively still for five to 10 minutes.

safety heart rate—The heart rate prescribed for beginning exercisers in any aerobic activity. This range is usually 60 percent or less of the maximum heart rate and represents the least amount of stress you can put on your heart and still receive a beneficial exercise effect.

steady state—Maintaining a given heart rate over a period of time.

stopwatch—A watch that can be started and stopped to time activities.

strength—Maximum force or tension that a muscle can produce against resistance.

stress—Nonspecific response of the body to any demands made on it.

stress response—Physical reaction to a stimulus (stressor).

stressor—Any physical, psychological, or environmental event or condition that initiates the stress response.

stroke volume—Amount of blood ejected by the heart in one beat (contraction).

submaximum heart rate test—An assessment below your maximum heart rate to predict (estimate) your maximum heart rate.

target heart rate zone—Optimum intensity range for aerobic exercise. Also known as the training zone.

target zone—This monitor feature allows you to set the top and/or bottom for a range of heartbeats you wish to measure. If your heart rate is below or above either of these two limits, a warning beep will sound with each heartbeat and, in some models, the display will flash. Also known as training zone.

time functions—The different type of timing features that a watch provides, such as the ability to display time of day or the ability to serve as a stopwatch.

timers—Some monitor models allow you to set an audible timer that will beep or "chirp" at a specific time in your workout. For example, you can set a timer to sound off every 30 minutes.

total recovery heart rate—The time it takes for your heart rate to return to the pre-exercise level after cessation of exercise.

training—Any sustained cardiovascular exercise at a heart rate or intensity level sufficient to result in metabolic adaptation in the muscles involved. The commonly accepted lower threshold or floor for training is considered to be 50 percent of maximum heart rate.

training tree—A type of training model based on progressively increasing or decreasing training load.

training zone—This feature allows you to set high and low limits for a range of heartbeats called a heart zone. Also known as target zone.

wellness—Engaging in attitudes and behaviors that enhance quality of life and maximize personal potential.

AN INTRODUCTION TO HEART ZONE TRAINING

Unit Objective

In this unit, the teacher will find the background information needed to present Heart Zone Training (HZT) to students.

Unit Outline

Notes to the Teacher

Biomechanics of the Heart

Facts About the Five Heart Zones

Notes to the Teacher

Our goal is to provide the educator with a fitness curriculum that will enhance a learner's ability to make responsible decisions regarding a healthy lifestyle. This curriculum provides tools to help students take an active role in maintaining and improving their health, while augmenting the current curriculum with the latest technology trends.

Keeping a record of their personal data and reflecting on the experience will help students maximize their learning. A journal page master has been provided for this purpose (see appendix G).

Each unit in this curriculum includes the following:

- Background information
- Lesson outlines
- Reproducible student worksheets

This curriculum uses new technology—a heart rate monitor—to monitor, assess, and manage health. Before you introduce this curriculum, it is important that you familiarize yourself with the monitor that you will be using in class, particularly if it has multiple functions. Although there are many similarities among the different models, individual functions and programming processes vary. Be sure to rehearse the procedure for distributing and collecting monitors. We suggest you use an HZT "checkout station" for this purpose. The checkout station is a hanging unit with 20 clear pocket divisions, which make it easy to check the status of the equipment.

Here are some helpful suggestions for managing equipment:

- Use the heart rate monitor checkout station and name card identification for each student. If your students are regularly assigned a mailbox number, this also works well for identification.
- Use a check-in policy that includes an alcohol swab of the chest strap and clearing the memory function from monitors, so the next class can begin immediately.
- Depending on the number of classes in which the monitor is used, the monitor distribution process can be simplified if each student is assigned a specific monitor, much like checking out a textbook.
- In some class situations, the activities will be more successful if students partner with one another and one student wears the chest strap and the second wears a

monitor only and does the record keeping. (Note: only the student wearing the chest strap will receive a heart rate readout.) The activity can be repeated and the roles of the students reversed.

It is advantageous for the classroom set of monitors to all be of the same brand and model.

Biomechanics of the Heart

Before we get into the dynamics of Heart Zone Training and its applications for your school program, we need to take a look at a couple of machines that are key to HZT success. One is electronic—the heart rate monitor; the other, organic—the heart.

Your heart, a muscle, is a pump that in a grown person is approximately the size of a human fist. Its purpose is to pump blood throughout the body. The pumping action used to describe how the heart works is much like the opening and closing of a fist, so this motion is an excellent way to visualize how the heart works. The heart "works" by continually and repeatedly expanding to allow blood to flow into the heart, then contracting to push blood to flow out of the heart.

The complete heartbeat sequence is somewhat like a musical rhythm. The rhythm consists of a sequence of electrical activities beginning at the sinoatrial node—the pacemaker of the heart located in its upper right side. This pacemaker is a bundle of specialized nerve tissue that receives regulating messages from your brain. If your cells need more fuel or more oxygen, the brain automatically speeds up the contraction rate of the pump, which increases the blood flow.

Although we talk about the heart as a single pump, it is actually two pumps separated in the center to the right and left sides of the heart by a septum in much the same way the septum in the nose separates the two sides of the nose. Each side of the heart has two chambers joined together by valves. The receiving chamber is called the atrium. The pumping chamber is called the ventricle.

Throughout the contraction phase, blood is pumped out of the heart. During the relaxation phase of the rhythm, there is time for the blood to refill the chambers between beats.

The right side receives carbon dioxide-rich blood that is returning from different parts of the body in a chamber called the right atrium. During the cycle of contraction, this blood flows from the atrium through a one-way valve that prevents the blood from flowing backward, to a second heart chamber, the right ventricle. It then is pumped to the lungs from the ventricle.

While blood flows through the lungs, it releases the stored carbon dioxide waste gases it acquired from blood cells that used up oxygen-rich blood, then the red blood corpuscles absorb atmospheric oxygen that you've inhaled while breathing. This oxygen-filled blood flows from the lungs to the left atrium. From there it flows through a one-way valve to the left ventricle, which pumps the blood to arteries that distribute it to all parts of the body.

Most people think the heart is located just left of the center of your body. In fact, it's nearly in the center of the chest. The average heart weighs less than a pound, yet it manages to efficiently pump blood with incredible force. If you measured the power from your heart's 40 million beats per year, it would equal a force capable of lifting you 100 miles above the Earth. For someone of average fitness level, the volume and water pressure of a kitchen faucet at full blast fall short of what a heart working maximally can do.

Look at the diagram of the heart in figure I.1a and b. Each time your heart "beats," what it's really doing is going through one cycle of contraction and relaxation. The heart tells itself to do this by sending itself an electrical message. As the heartbeat begins, a positive electrical charge spreads across the cell membranes. Then, there's a sudden change—the heart sends itself a negative charge that makes it contract. The heart's electrical change from the positive to the negative state is one heartbeat, and this electrical activity is what heart rate monitors (and electrocardiographs) measure, allowing them to record your heartbeats very accurately.

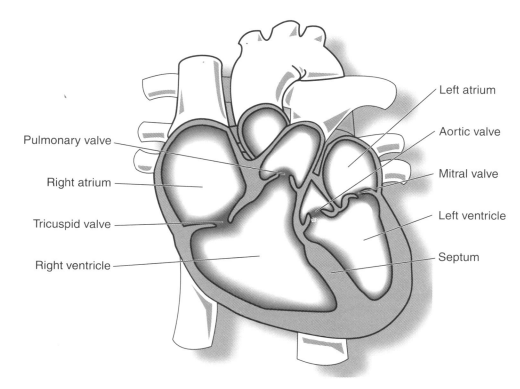

Pulmonary valve

Right atrium

Tricuspid valve

Right ventricle

Left atrium

Aortic valve

Mitral valve

Left ventricle

Septum

Figure I.1a   Chambers of the heart.

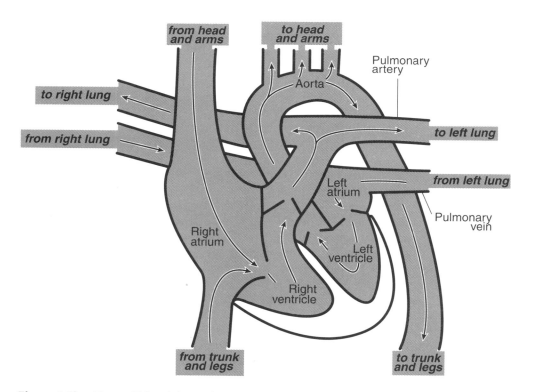

from head
and arms

to head
and arms

to right lung

from right lung

Aorta

Pulmonary
artery

to left lung

from left lung

Left
atrium

Pulmonary
vein

Right
atrium

Left
ventricle

Right
ventricle

from trunk
and legs

to trunk
and legs

Figure I.1b   Flow of blood through the heart.

Drawings courtesy of the American Heart Association.

The Heart: Pumps and Polarizations

A basic idea that most of us have about the heart is that it is a pump, but really it's two pumps, two sides, in one. Each pump, or side, of the heart has three valves: (1) ingoing, dividing the outside of the heart from the first, upper chamber; (2) interior, dividing the upper and lower chambers on each side from one another; and (3) outgoing, dividing the lower chamber from the outside of the heart.

The pump on the right side of the heart receives returning, or "venous," blood from all parts of the body. The first right-hand chamber (the right atrium) fills and then quickly passes about a cupful or so of blood with each stroke. The blood goes through the interior valve into the lower chamber (the right ventricle), which is much larger and more powerful. The right ventricle then ejects the blood up to the lungs for carbon dioxide off-loading and oxygen on-loading. The same cupful of blood returns from the lungs and enters the top half of the left-side pump—the left atrium. The heart takes a brief rest while the atrium fills—it takes time for the muscle to contract and eject the blood. From the left atrium, the left interior valve passes the blood to the last chamber, the left ventricle, which is the largest of all of the heart chambers and which jettisons the blood out through the aorta, and from there to the rest of the body.

The coordination of two pumps, four chambers, and six valves is one of those wondrous activities of the nervous system, orchestrated via chemical transmitters and electrical impulses. Interestingly, most of the time the cardiac muscle is on its own. It independently creates its own electrical signals without any signals from the brain, rhythmically beating away until there's an order to make a change.

The communication signal for the cardiac muscle to contract begins at the sinoatrial (S-A) node. The S-A node independently and rhythmically sends out an electrical message from inside the upper part of the right atrium. This message instructs the atria to contract, and they do so concurrently, ejecting blood down into the ventricles. This S-A message is the depolarization phase of the upper chambers. As the message arrives at the doorstep of the atrial-ventricular node (A-V node), located on the inside of the same chamber and near the center of the heart muscle, the A-V node sends out a second signal. This is the depolarization of the ventricle muscles. The A-V node alerts the two bottom chambers, the ventricles, to contract. All of this is timed perfectly. After the upper two chambers contract, there is a delay of about .13 seconds for the message to be sent from the S-A to the A-V node. This timing is critical—it's the time the heart muscle uses to squeeze the blood out of the upper chambers and into the lower chambers.

The A-V node is a ball of special muscle cells extending out of the right atrium like a lead wire running down the inside center of the heart and breaking apart into branches (called Bundle branches). When the A-V node extension wire reaches the lower ventricle chambers, it branches again and then it branches some more until the branches permeate uniformly to the two lower chambers. This branching is important because it allows the message to travel quickly to all parts of the lower chambers so that when the muscles contract, they do so as one unit and not sequentially. This allows for more complete expulsion of all of the blood from the chamber.

This contraction represents one heartbeat. The heart pumps blood through the body with a series of continuous contractions. This effort is measured as beats per minute (bpm). Assuming an average of about 70 bpm, the heart contracts about 100,000 times every 24 hours.

Consider the fact that the heart and its pumping system, which scientists have attempted to duplicate without success, pump six quarts of blood through more than 96,000 miles of blood vessels. This is the equivalent of 6,300 gallons being pumped per day. That is almost 115 million gallons in only 50 years.

The six quarts of blood are made up of more than 24 trillion cells that make 3,000 to 5,000 trips through the body every day. Seven million new blood cells are produced every second! This pumping system has the capability of working nonstop for decades without missing a beat.

Heart Rates

Heart rates (HR) vary tremendously among individuals. Resting heart rates can vary as much as 30 to 40 beats between two people of the same height, weight, and age. They also vary between the sexes because the female heart is smaller in size. Women average about 5 to 7 bpm higher than men do, because their heart is smaller in size and mass.

Your resting heart rate is the number of times your heart beats in one minute when you are at complete, uninterrupted rest. As most people get fit, their resting heart rate will get lower. Sedentary, unfit people typically have higher resting heart rates. Exercise can make your heart more efficient and accomplish its work at a lower rate.

The cardiac output of the heart is based on how often the heart beats per minute (HR) and how much blood there is being pumped (stroke volume or SV). The total cardiac output formula is simple: Cardiac Output = HR × SV.

Before we can get very far into zone training, we need to understand heart zones and the differences between them. There are some special characteristics of the five heart zones that make them what they are. The key fact is that a different thing happens in each of the different heart zones. This means that you have to train in different zones to get each of the different benefits.

Facts About the Five Heart Zones

Fact 1: Zones have size. The size of each zone is a 10 percent range of your true maximum heart rate (Max HR). The size of the zone in number of beats depends on how high your true Max HR is. Given a 200 bpm Max HR (which is very convenient for multiplying), each of the five zones would be 10 percent of 200, or 20 beats wide. Zones for most people range from 15 to 20 beats in size; this is big enough to allow for some "wiggle room" when you are working out, but small enough to be on target for your particular training goal(s).

Fact 2: Zones have structure. A zone may be viewed as being made up of two different parts: its top and bottom halves. In other words, inside every zone are an upper and a lower zone. So, while the whole "Aerobic" zone may be from 70 to 80 percent of your Max HR, the lower half of the zone is 70 to 75 percent (or 140 to 150 bpm in our 200 bpm Max HR example), and the upper Aerobic zone is 75 to 80 percent (or 150 to 160 bpm in this case). It's just a way to subdivide a heart zone into two smaller, even more focused parts.

Fact 3: Zones have dividing lines. The upper and lower limits of each zone coincide with the floor and ceiling of its bordering zones. The floor or bottom of the Aerobic zone, for example, is 70 percent of your Max HR. This floor or lower limit is that heart rate where you first break into this zone. The Aerobic zone ceiling, 80 percent Max HR, is the line at the very top or threshold of the zone. At this point you are passing through the Aerobic zone ceiling into the floor of the next higher and more intense zone, the "Threshold" zone.

Fact 4: Zone names correspond with their benefits. Each zone has a specific benefit that comes from the physiological activities that happen when you exercise within that heart rate zone. For example, the "Z1 Healthy Heart" zone is exactly that, the range of heart rates where most individuals realize the most cardiovascular benefits, leading to improved heart and lung function.

Fact 5: Zones have numbers. There are certain specific and measurable events that are so exact that they're represented by a single heartbeat value called a heart rate number. You may already know a few of them: the maximum heart rate number and the resting heart rate number are specific heart rate numbers that are located in relationship to (inside or on the dividing lines of) the zones. For example, chart I.1 shows the location of your Max HR on the ceiling of zone 5.

HEART ZONE TRAINING®

Heart Zones Education

Training Zone (% maximum heart rate)	Fuel Burning	Max HR 150	Max HR 155	Max HR 160	Max HR 165	Max HR 170	Max HR 175	Max HR 180	Max HR 185	Max HR 190	Max HR 195	Max HR 200	Max HR 205	Max HR 210	Max HR 215	Max HR 220
Z5 RED LINE 90%-100%	GLYCOGEN BURNING	150	155	160	165	170	175	180	185	190	195	200	205	210	215	220
		135	140	144	149	153	158	162	167	171	176	180	185	189	194	198
Z4 THRESHOLD 80%-90%		135	140	144	149	153	158	162	167	171	176	180	185	189	194	198
		120	124	128	132	136	140	144	148	152	156	160	164	168	172	176
Z3 AEROBIC 70%-80%		120	124	128	132	136	140	144	148	152	156	160	164	168	172	176
		105	109	112	116	119	123	126	130	133	137	140	144	147	151	154
Z2 TEMPERATE 60%-70%	FAT BURNING	105	109	112	116	119	123	126	130	133	137	140	144	147	151	154
		90	93	96	99	102	105	108	111	114	117	120	123	126	129	132
Z1 HEALTHY HEART 50%-60%		90	93	96	99	102	105	108	111	114	117	120	123	126	129	132
		75	78	80	83	85	88	90	93	95	98	100	103	105	108	110

Chart I.1 Heart Zone Training chart.

To read the Heart Zone Training chart, do the following:

- Find your maximum heart rate across the top row of the chart.
- Next, follow the column down from your Max HR to find your five zone ranges.
- Note that the floor of one zone is the ceiling of the zone below it.

From Middle School Healthy Hearts in the Zone: A Heart Rate Monitoring Program for Lifelong Fitness by Deve Swaim and Sally Edwards, 2002, Human Kinetics, Champaign, IL.

UNIT II

USING HEART RATE MONITORS

Unit Objective

A heart rate monitor provides the challenge to apply technology to self-awareness of the heart's function. In this module, students will be introduced to the use of the heart rate monitor and to the five heart zones.

Unit Outline

What Is a Heart Rate Monitor?

All About the Five Heart Zones

Lesson Plans and Student Worksheets

 A heart rate monitor provides a window inside the body.

What Is a Heart Rate Monitor?

Heart rate monitors were in the realm of science fiction not so very long ago. Around 1912, researchers started using water buckets as counterweights in the first laboratory model of a heart rate monitoring device. The first electronic heart-monitoring tool, the electrocardiograph, was originally the size of a room. Current models are more sophisticated, yet they still are not portable. Thankfully, we now have the personal heart rate monitor. It may not do everything the electrocardiograph in your doctor's office does, but it does very nicely fill the needs of anyone who wants to accurately measure his heart rate. Today's heart rate monitors are the size of a wristwatch at the price of a pair of top athletic shoes. All heart rate monitors currently require the use of a chest strap. Tomorrow, the heart rate monitor's computer electronics may integrate into a small, fashion-smart watch with no electrode-bearing chest strap.

A heart rate monitor gives us biofeedback about the heart. It accurately reports the average of the number of times your heart contracts in one minute by picking up the electrical signals given off by the heart, then transmitting the information to a monitor typically worn on a wrist. A heart rate monitor measures relative exercise intensity.

The terms "heart rate monitor" and "heart rate watch" are synonymous. Most, but not all, monitors are watches. The monitor itself is the receiving unit that collects the data transmitted from the chest strap and processes it using a computer chip to calculate a heart rate number. This number is updated every three to five seconds. The first few numbers that appear on your watch should be ignored, because the software inside the computer needs enough sample heart rates to accurately calculate a value. Likewise, if you quickly accelerate or decelerate, your heart rate values will always be slightly lagging behind your real heart rate number.

There are three components to all heart rate monitors: a chest belt, a transmitter, and a receiver or wrist monitor. Some models of heart rate monitors have only two components because the chest belt and transmitter have been combined.

The chest belt: This adjustable elastic belt is worn snugly around the chest, usually just below the nipple line. Attached to the elastic chest strap is the transmitter unit. The transmitter receives the data from our heart through its electrodes, processes it, and then transmits it to the monitor.

The transmitter: The transmitter either snaps or connects onto the chest belt or is a part of the chest belt. The transmitter picks up the electrical signal and translates it into data that can be sent to the wrist monitor via an electromagnetic field, similar to a radio wave.

The wrist monitor: The wrist monitor looks like a wristwatch and functions as the receiver of the transmitter's signals. Different wrist monitors give different displays, but the basics are all the same—they display heart rate in beats per minute (bpm), as shown in figure II.1.

Not all monitors have all the features shown here—but all have some variation of these features. Normally, the more features, the more expensive the monitor. All heart rate monitors, though, will work with the Heart Zone Training system presented here.

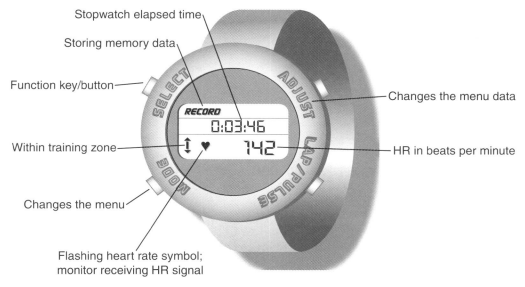

Figure II.1 Wrist monitor.

All About the Five Heart Zones

There are five different heart zones that are each 10 percent of an individual's personal maximum heart rate (Max HR). Students train in different zones on different days to accomplish their fitness goals. Each of the different heart zones has its own unique nature.

The Z1 Healthy Heart Zone

Being at the easiest, most comfortable intensity range—50 to 60 percent Max HR—the "Healthy Heart" zone has taken some hard knocks from many fitness professionals. For years, many have said that there's simply no benefit to exercising in this zone, because there is no improvement in the body's oxygen utilization. However, there is noticeable improvement in several other wellness categories: the blood pressure lowers, cholesterol levels improve, body fat decreases or stabilizes, and muscle mass increases.

If you walk two miles a day for 30 minutes, three times a week, death from all-cause morbidity is re-duced by 55 percent, according to Ken Cooper, MD.

These are the reasons to work out in the Healthy Heart zone—because you want to get healthier. If your goal is to be a competitive athlete, you probably will only spend time warming up and cooling down in this zone. If your interests are to improve your health, especially if you are just starting a fitness program, the Healthy Heart zone is the place to be.

The zone floor for the Healthy Heart zone is 50 percent of your Max HR. When you cross this floor, you will realize health benefits. The amount of energy burned during this time will not be as great as in higher zones, but you will be burning a relatively large percentage of the type of calories that are most preferred as your source of fuel—fat. There's a critical, but not much discussed, difference between total calories burned and the type of calories burned. Quality, or type of calories burned, is just as important as the quantity, the total number of calories expended in a workout. In the Healthy Heart zone, while the total calories burned per workout may be low, a very large percentage of the calories are fat calories. Carbohydrates are high-grade fuels, perfect for burning in the higher training zones. Table II.1 summarizes the events and conditions within Z1.

Table II.1
Fuel Usage: Healthy Heart ZI

Zone	Zone name	% Max HR	Fuels burned	Energy expended*
Z1	Healthy Heart	50–60%	10% carbohydrates 50–75% fat 5% protein	±5 calories per minute

*Energy expenditure varies among individuals.

The Healthy Heart zone is a very comfortable level of exercise—you get the feeling that you could go on forever. The average number of calories burned per minute (about three to six) is lower than in any other zone, though. So, if your number-one goal is not basic cardiovascular fitness, but fat loss, you'll need to move up to a zone that burns more total calories.

The overweight person has one thing in his favor when he starts a fitness plan—the heavier he is, the more calories he burns per minute of exercise.

Even for students with more advanced fitness goals, the Z1 Healthy Heart zone is a good place to start, as well as to come back to from time to time when needing a break from more strenuous workouts.

The Z2 Temperate Zone

The "Z2 Temperate" zone is so-called because it is a moderate and comfortable zone. As in the Healthy Heart zone, approximately 50 to 75 percent of all of the calories that are burned in the Z2 zone come from fat. However, unlike the approximately four to six calories per minute you can expect to burn in the Healthy Heart zone, in the Temperate zone an average person will burn about 5 to 8 calories per minute! So, in 10 minutes of exercise, depending on body weight and other factors, a person will burn about 100 calories, and of these, approximately 50-75 will be from fat. This blend or ratios of fuels will change to some degree based on diet and current fitness. Table II.2 summarizes the events and conditions within Z2.

Table II.2
Fuel Usage: Temperate Z2

Zone	Zone name	% Max HR	Fuels burned	Energy expended*
Z2	Temperate	60–70%	10% carbohydrates 50-75% fat 5% protein	± 5-8 calories per minute

*Energy expenditure varies among individuals.

Continuing to train in higher zones will burn more calories, and it also will burn proportionately less fat as a percentage of the total calories.

 Fat is our most abundant energy source. It is approximately 50 times more abundant in our bodies than carbohydrates.

When you exercise in the Temperate zone, your health rewards are doubled because you dispose of more body fat and, at the same time, gain muscle mass. Consequently, there is more muscle available to burn fat and the resting metabolic rate increases more. In other words, the more muscle mass you have, the more calories you'll burn just sitting still.

The Z3 Aerobic Zone

In the "Aerobic" zone you'll get the most benefits in the least amount of time. It gets you fitter, gets you faster, and gets you thinner. That's why it's been touted for decades as the guts of the one mythical "target zone." The Aerobic zone might be the heart of the heart of it. Table II.3 illustrates some of the events and activities in Z3.

Table II.3
Fuel Usage: Aerobic Z3

Zone	Zone name	% Max HR	Fuels burned	Energy expended*
Z3	Aerobic	70–80%	60% carbohydrates 35% fat 5% protein	± 8-10 calories per minute

*Energy expenditure varies among individuals.

The Aerobic zone is the fitness area at the heart of the wellness continuum. It is the transition zone between the two health zones and the two performance zones. It's also the first of the zones in which performance training effects begin. In the Aerobic zone you begin to realize the changes that lead to athletic conditioning versus basic health and fitness.

Following are some of the cardiovascular improvements that your body undergoes as a result of aerobic exercise:

- An increase in the number and size of blood vessels, resulting in

    increased blood delivery to your muscles,

    increased oxygen delivery to the muscles for fuel,

    increased oxygen delivery to the fat cells to free them into the blood,

    increased blood to carry the fat from fat cells to the muscles,

    increased number of mitochondria within muscle cells that convert fuels for muscle combustion,

    increased size of each individual mitochondrion,

    increased number of capillaries in the working muscles,

    increased size of existing capillaries,

    increased size of coronary arteries, and

    reduction in blood pressure

- An increase in both the size and strength of the heart, resulting in

    increased stroke volume (the amount of blood pumped with each heartbeat),

    increased cardiac output (stroke volume times heart rate), and

    decreased heart rate for the same intensity level workload

- An increase in red blood cell volume, plasma volume, and total blood volume

Some of the cardiopulmonary or respiratory changes that result from training in the Aerobic zone include the following:

- Increased vital capacity (the amount of air that can be breathed out after a maximal intake of breath)

- Decreased respiratory rate (the number of breaths you take in response to a given level of workload)

- Increased maximal pulmonary ventilation (the volume of oxygen per minute you can breathe)

- Increased pulmonary diffusion (the amount of oxygen exchanged by the lungs)

- Increased difference in arterial-venous oxygen (the blood returning to the heart has a lower concentration of oxygen because of better oxygen extraction at the tissue level and better distribution of blood with more going to the working tissues and less to the more inactive tissues)

The Z4 Threshold Zone

This is a zone you're no doubt familiar with, though maybe you are unfamiliar with its name. Here's a hint: This is also known as the "shortness of breath" zone. Sound familiar? It's the zone where you cross over the threshold to burning more carbohydrates than fat and using more oxygen than is available.

It is called the "Threshold" zone because, for most fit people, within this zone of 80 to 90 percent Max HR is their anaerobic threshold. This is where you pass from aerobic metabolism, which means "with oxygen," to anaerobic metabolism, meaning "without oxygen." Above the anaerobic threshold, oxygen debt starts to rapidly accumulate and lactates are spewing out—it can be a very uncomfortable place. But here's the startling part about the anaerobic threshold: In unfit individuals, it is common to see anaerobic thresholds at around 60 to 70 percent of their Max HR. And in the extremely fit, it is common to see anaerobic thresholds above 90 percent of their Max HR. Table II.4 gives you a view of the parts of Z4.

Table II.4
Fuel Usage: Threshold Z4

Zone	Zone name	% Max HR	Fuels burned	Energy expended*
Z4	Threshold	80–90%	up to 80% carbohydrates 15-45% fat 5% protein	± 10-15 calories per minute

*Energy expenditure varies among individuals.

This is very important: If you are unfit and your anaerobic threshold heart rate point is within your low heart zones, you can't train very long in the Threshold zone. It's simply too high a heart rate intensity. You need to stay below your anaerobic threshold for all of your exercise; hence, the Healthy Heart zone or Temperate zone is perfect. This is one of the reasons why exercise fails the healthy unfit: We're asking them to train too far above their anaerobic thresholds. This is a key factor in helping kids develop productive exercise programs.

The Z5 Red line Zone

The "Red line" zone, with heart rates from 90 to 100 percent of your Max HR, is the challenge zone for athletic or high fitness development.

No one can hang out for long periods of time in the Red line zone. Your heart rate cannot stay at or near maximum, because of its exceedingly high demand for fuels. Every second you are in the Red line zone, your body's oxygen and glycogen needs exceed your ability to deliver them. The heart muscle is a "work now, pay now" muscle, and it will not go into oxygen debt. Because skeletal muscles operate under the principle of "work now, pay later," they have the ability to keep on going, past the threshold point, and drive themselves into oxygen and glycogen debt.

Why do we use our Max HR number as the anchor point for zones rather than our anaerobic or lactate threshold? We do this because Max HR is a fixed number, so we can fix the five zones. Your anaerobic threshold heart rate changes with conditioning, so as you get fitter, it goes higher. Because your anaerobic threshold heart rate number moves with conditioning, all of your zones also change with conditioning. With each beat of change in anaerobic heart rate, there is a change in all the floors and ceilings of all the zones. It is, therefore, more practical and less confusing to use Max HR as the anchor point.

One of the most frequently asked questions about Heart Zone Training applies here: Are the benefits cumulative? In other words, if you hang out in Z5, are you going to get all of the benefits from the Healthy Heart, Temperate, Aerobic, and Threshold zones? The answer is no. In each zone, a different process occurs that is specific to that process; if you want to receive that benefit, then you have to pay your dues in that zone.

Table II.5 gives you an overview of Z5.

Table II.5
Fuel Usage: Redline Z5

Zone	Zone name	% Max HR	Fuels burned	Energy expended*
Z5	Redline	90–100%	90% carbohydrates 5% protein 5% fat	± 15-18 calories per minute

*Energy expenditure varies among individuals.

Exercise results in emotional and physical benefits. These benefits can be further enhanced by having students exercise within the heart zones that best fit their goals.

Lesson Plans

Now we're ready to start using the heart rate monitor (HRM) to gather data on individual heart rate response. Following are a series of lessons to aid students in understanding their heart and to introduce them to Heart Zone Training.

Lesson II.1   Using a Heart Rate Monitor—Functions and Ambient Heart Rate

A heart rate monitor is a wristwatch-size piece of advanced technological equipment that measures the electrical impulses that cause your heart to beat. With a HRM you can observe your heart at work or rest and continuously note its response to stimuli.

Outcomes

- Students will learn the vocabulary terms associated with heart rate monitors.
- Students will use HRM to determine their ambient heart rate.

Materials

- HRM for each learner
- Overheads of functions
- "Using a Heart Rate Monitor" worksheet on pages 28-29

 Since the students will be recording their ambient heart rates at various times during this lesson, have them remain in their seats throughout the lesson.

Activity

1. Explain the checkout system and have the students check out a monitor.
2. Identify and name the parts of the HRM:
   - Wrist monitor
   - Chest strap
   - Transmitter
3. Explain and, if possible, demonstrate how to wear a HRM, then have the students put them on following the steps listed.
4. Identify the function keys and teach the students the proper mechanics for getting a heart rate readout on their monitors. For most multifunction monitors, you can change functions by pressing and holding the "mode" key until the flashing heart icon appears in the display.
5. Pass out the worksheet for using a HRM.
6. Have students record their current heart rate on line A on their worksheet. Define this (to students) as their ambient heart rate.
7. Have students write a definition of "ambient." (It is the number of beats your heart contracts per minute when you are awake but in a sedentary and stationary position, such as sitting at your desk. Healthy norms range between 50 and 80 bpm.)
8. Have the students record their ambient heart rate on line B.
9. Have them find their average ambient heart rate for this period by adding all their readings and dividing that total by the number of readings.
10. Check for understanding that there is no "right" ambient heart rate. What kinds of things could contribute to the different heart rates in class? (Hunger, sleepiness, fatigue, anger, joy, temperature, stress, fitness.)

Putting on a Heart Rate Monitor

1. Put on your chest strap and transmitter. The transmitter needs to be centered over the chest, next to the skin, and with the manufacturer's logo right side up.

2. To assure the monitor picks up the signal, moisten the electrodes on the underside of the transmitter with a saline solution. (Saliva is a saline solution!) The electrodes on the transmitter go against the skin.

3. Adjust the chest strap so that it will fit snugly around your chest. Most people find it useful to put the strap around the waist as though it were a belt. When the chest strap is pulled up around the chest, it should be centered and positioned below the breasts and be snug enough to hold.

4. The most satisfactory way to wear an HRM chest strap is so that it's in direct contact with the skin. Some chest transmitters will work over a lightweight shirt but the shirt will need to be moistened to enhance recognition of the signal.

5. Place the monitor on the wrist so that it is easy to see. To do so, set the monitor so that it displays your heart rate.

6. Record your heart rate after one to two minutes of wearing the monitor to allow time for it to accurately determine heart rate.

Because monitors pick up electrical signals, have students maintain a distance of three feet from others wearing transmitters in order to prevent "cross talk." For additional troubleshooting refer to appendix B.

Assessment

Have the students draw a diagram of their HRM and identify the function keys and the steps necessary to get a display of their heart rate. Follow the manufacturer's user manual for specific details for each monitor.

Lesson II.2   Taking Your Pulse

The purpose of this instruction is twofold: first, to familiarize students with the proper way to manually monitor their pulse; and second, to demonstrate the improved accuracy and ease of monitoring their heart rate with a HRM.

Outcome

Students will demonstrate their ability to take their pulse manually at different sites on the body.

Materials

- HRM
- "Pulse Rate—Heart Rate" worksheet on page 30

Importance of Measuring Heart Rate

Long before we had the tools to listen to and measure our heart rate, medical professionals were paying attention to the beat of the heart. In fact, the manner in which the heart beats, fast or slow or regular or irregular, is so important that it is one of the first things the doctor checks when we get a medical exam.

Basically, there are two methods of measuring heart rate: manually (with your fingers), which is commonly called "palpation," or electronically (with a heart rate monitor).

Although it makes sense that the heart rate and pulse rate should be identical, in practice there is a difference. Heart rate refers to the electrical impulses that cause your heart to beat, but pulse rate refers only to the movement of blood through your arteries. There can be a number of factors that would interfere with blood flow prior to reaching the site for palpation; it stands to reason that the farther away from the heart a heart rate is monitored, the weaker the signal. In addition, the human error in counting pulse rate has been shown to be significant. In one study, people monitoring their pulse by palpation reported a reading that averaged 17 beats per minute lower than the reading that was taken at the same time with a heart rate monitor.

The pulse or heart rate can differ greatly between two people of the same age. This difference is a combination of genetic and heart size differences.

Feeling Your Pulse

With proper attention and training, almost anybody can learn to "feel" a pulse. In this lesson the student will practice taking a pulse rate manually (palpation) and then compare the rate to that shown on a heart rate monitor.

It's suggested that the sites used in this session be brachial (at the wrist) and carotid (at the neck) (see figure II.1 a and b). When teaching students how to take a carotid pulse, be sure to remind them *not* to exert pressure against the artery. Pressure at that point can stimulate the vagus nerve, which can cause a person to feel faint.

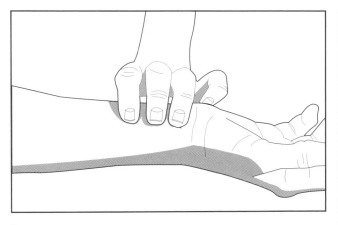

a   b

Figure II.1   Two locations to take a pulse: *(a)* brachial and *(b)* carotid.

Although there are as many as 16 sites on the body (more about this later), the most common places to monitor a pulse are the following:

- *At the carotid artery.* Place two fingers lightly on the side of your neck just below your chin.
- *At the brachial artery on the wrist.* Place two fingers lightly on the inside of your wrist below your thumb.

Once the students have learned how to monitor their heart rate manually and with their HRM, the two methods can be compared and contrasted.

Activity

1. Teach students how to find their pulse at the brachial or carotid artery. Words that are useful to help students understand what they are searching for are "pulse," "jet" (of blood), "jump," and "surge." Demonstrate the positions. Explain that they should be able to feel the surge of blood that occurs when the blood is pumped past a place where an artery, which carries blood away from the heart, is close to the surface of the skin. The number of times the artery surges or pulses in a minute is their pulse rate, measured in beats per minute.

2. Ask the students to count the number of beats for six seconds (you will monitor the time for the class)

and multiply that number by 10 to find out the number of beats in 60 seconds or one minute. [Remind them that six (seconds) $\times$ 10 (the multiple) = 60 seconds or one minute.]

3. Have the students repeat the activity several times to assure they are comfortable with the procedure at each site.

4. Have them put on their HRM and then set it so that their heart rate is displayed. (Remind them to keep three feet of distance between themselves and all other students so that another transmitter won't affect the readings for cross talk.)

5. Now ask the students to take their pulse manually once more and immediately compare it to the monitor readout. Repeat this several times. It's unusual that the two readings are the same because it takes a very highly skilled person to take an accurate pulse manually. Have them record two of these pulse and heart rate readings on their worksheets.

6. Involve the students in some movement for two- to five-minute periods (so their pulse will elevate). Ask them to note their heart rate on their monitor and with palpation. Ask them to compare the two readings and record them as the third rate on their worksheets.

Assessment

Discuss what happened during the student exercises. Ask the students to write their reflections on their worksheets:

Did they get the same reading manually and on the monitor?

Discuss what could have caused the differences:

- An error in accuracy of manually counting their heart rate.
- An error in math.
- An error in stopping their activity to take their "activity" pulse. As soon as they stop movement, their heart rate begins to recover to the pre-exercise level.

Homework

The "Resting Heart Rate" worksheet on page 31

Extension

Tell the students that although the brachial and carotid are the most common places that we feel for a pulse, there are 16 sites on the body where the artery is close enough to the surface of the skin that the pulse can be felt (table II.6).

The ease of finding and recording a pulse at each of these sites varies from person to person. The best way to find a pulse is to press an artery against a bone and feel for the pulsation. *Never* press hard!

Table II.6
Sites to Use for Manual Measurement of Heart Rate

Site	Number of sites
Carotid	2
Radial—shoulder	2
Radial—elbow	2
Radial—wrist	2
Femoral—groin	2
Plantar—on top of foot	2
Posterior tibia (near anklebone)	2
At the temple in front of ear	2

Lesson II.3   The Amazing Body

The heart muscle is invisible to the naked eye. Seeing the actual heart muscle contract is possible in the video *The Universe Within*. Presented by NOVA, the video takes you inside the human body and shows how bones and muscles and the digestion and other systems function.

Outcome

Students will know key terminology associated with the heart.

Materials

- HRM
- NOVA film, *The Universe Within*
- "Heart Diagram" worksheet on page 32
- "Family Story" worksheet on page 33

Human Body Video

The Universe Within shows how superstar athletes use their bodies to reach their limits and it demonstrates how all the systems of the body work in unison to make all that we do possible.

The film progresses through the functions of the bones and muscles; then the heart portion of the film begins approximately 12 to 15 minutes into the film. The heart functions portion begins with champion long jumper Mike Powell saying, "As an athlete you have to know your body real well." He is standing at a high hurdle doing leg swings.

Although this video has been included in its full 90-minute format, which shows all the major body systems and how they interrelate to each other, you may want to show only the portion on the functions of the heart at this time. We suggest that you use the digestive portion later in the curriculum with the discussion on the impact of food on heart rate. As with any video, you should preview it before showing. (If you cannot find this video at your local library, it can be ordered from WGBH Boston Video, 125 Western Ave., Boston, MA 02134; **www.wgbh.org**.)

Activity

1. Give the students some background about the film. Tell them to observe their ambient heart rate as they watch and record this number periodically.

2. Have them note the terms they hear that have relationship to the function of the heart.

3. After viewing, as a class, complete the "Heart Diagram" worksheet, identifying the chambers and major arteries and veins.

4. Next, ask the students, "What scenes in the video most affected you? Why?" Have them write a short paper on this.

5. When they have completed their papers, ask them to share.

Homework

Have each student interview a family member or friend about heart disease, using the "Family Story" worksheet. Did they suffer a heart attack or have open-heart surgery? What could have prevented these? What kinds of lifestyle changes occurred as a result?

Lesson II.4   Delta Heart Rate

Delta is a Greek term for "change" and is written as a triangle. For the purposes of this lesson, delta heart rate (ΔHR), also known as an "orthostatic test," measures the "change" that occurs when the students move from one position to another, in this case from a horizontal to a vertical position.

In fitness training (not applicable in this curriculum), a variation in the regular monitoring of a delta heart rate of more than 20 to 30 beats could be indicative of overtraining, stress, or pending immune compromise. The athlete who experiences this increase in ΔHR typically decreases the workout or does not exercise that day.

Once the students have mastered the skill of recording ΔHR, it is recommended that this reading be used as a daily activity during this unit. Students then have an opportunity to self-examine the stress that is going on in their life and why they may be experiencing a change in their ΔHR. It also gives them valuable practice at using the HRM.

Outcome

The students will apply a process for monitoring their heart's response to movement and recovery.

Materials

- HRM
- "Delta Heart Rate" worksheet on pages 34-35

Activity

1. Explain to the students that they are going to take a heart rate measure that demonstrates their heart's ability to respond to a change in body position.

2. Check out monitors and have half of the class put on chest straps and monitors, the other half of the class put on monitors only. Explain that they will monitor for each other—both monitors will read out the heart rate of the student with the chest strap. Partners want to stay in close proximity to one another.

3. Remind the students to keep a distance of three feet between receivers to prevent "cross talk" and ensure accurate results. They shouldn't get too close to other teams.

4. Talk to the class in a manner that relaxes them and clearly explain what is expected of each of the partners.

5. Ask students with the chest strap and transmitter to lie on the floor to start the activity. Their partner (with the monitor) should remain close (and within three feet of their prone partner's monitor) and observe that student's heart rate.

6. Manage the time intervals so that everyone is at the same stage together. Have the recording partner record heart rates (1) for the supine position, and (2) after standing for two minutes.

7. Repeat the activity with the roles reversed.

8. When everyone in class has their prone and standing heartbeat numbers, have them calculate their ΔHR and chart the results.

If you don't have enough monitors for every student, this can easily be done as outlined here, except that the person being tested wears the chest strap only. Her partner wears the monitor only. This allows the student with the monitor to receive her partner's heart rate data on the monitor watch that she is wearing.

Assessment

Have the students make a list of the kinds of things they could do to slow down or calm their heart rate. Have them think in terms of their senses. Discuss and create a list as a class. Remind them to refer to these the next time they take a delta heart measure.

Extension

Have students take a ΔHR reading through a variety of position changes (e.g., sitting/standing, laying/sitting).

Lesson II.5   Setting a Zone

There is a direct relationship between the emotional and physical load on the heart and the heart rate. During sleep the heart beats much more slowly than it does when one is awake. Add physical activity or stress and the heart rate increases. Heart rate is variable; it is not fixed or absolute. The following activity is designed to introduce students to the concept of "heart zones."

In fitness lingo a heart zone is a range of heartbeats per minute, for example, from 120 to 140 bpm. The top of a zone is called the ceiling. The bottom end of the zone is called the floor. If the heart rate were plotted in a series of heart zones, the ceiling of one zone would be the floor of another zone, and vice versa. There are five different zones, and we exercise in different zones to get different benefits.

As a health teacher you may be familiar with the term "target zone"—the pace at which people who exercise for aerobic benefits are encouraged to maintain their heart rate. However, this term is being faded out because there is no one target zone for aerobic benefit. There are multiple aerobic zones.

In the fitness industry it is now common to see a heart or target zone chart in which a maximum heart rate based on age is used to set a series of zones that accrue the benefits of exercising in that zone. These charts call the zones by various names. Typically, lower zones (intensities) have names such as "health" or "fat burning," "weight management" or "temperate." Midrange zones often are described as "aerobic" zones, and higher zones have names such as "anaerobic" or "competition." Finally at the highest intensity, there is "red line" or "hot zone." Sadly, these names have perpetuated misinformation about how the body works. Although we will not get into that in this activity, the heart zone concept is important for students to understand for the development of a Heart Zone Training program.

Heart Zone Training is based on the five heart zones:

Healthy Heart—an improvement in overall health, such as lowered blood pressure and lowered cholesterol

Temperate—increased fat burning and development of more muscle mass

Aerobic—strengthened cardiovascular endurance and extensive fat burning

Threshold—enhanced ability to achieve athletic results, including raised anaerobic threshold, oxygen-carrying capacity, and muscle mass

Red line—the high-performance zone, fastest and fittest

Outcomes

1. Students will understand the concept of zones.
2. Students will connect the zone concept to an exercise.

Materials

- HRM
- "Setting a Heart Zone" worksheet on page 36

Activity

1 Check out the heart rate monitors.

2. Have the students get a heart rate reading on their monitors and record their ambient heart rate.

3. Explain the concept of zones: that a zone is a range of heartbeats with the top of the zone called the ceiling and the bottom of the zone called the floor. Explain that different heart zones have different health and fitness benefits and that the students will learn more about those later.

4. Tell the students that they are going to attempt to keep their heart rate within a prescribed zone—do movement activities to keep their heart rate between the floor and ceiling of the prescribed zone.

5. To establish a zone, they will add 20 bpm to their ambient heart rate and label this the floor of the zone. Add 20 bpm to the floor number and call this the ceiling. Each student now has a "zone" measure based on her ambient heart rate. For example, for an ambient heart rate of 70 bpm, the floor of the zone would be plus 20, or 90 bpm, and the ceiling would be plus 20 bpm more, or 110 bpm. The "zone" would be 90 to 110 bpm.

6. Explain the process for setting a zone on a heart rate monitor. (See the instructions for your monitor model.) You may not want to enable the alarm on the first run-through.

7. After the monitors are programmed, have the students warm up sufficiently so that everyone's heart rate is in their zone.

8. Explain that they are to move sufficiently to keep their heart rate in this prescribed zone for three to five minutes. (Younger children should have a wider-range zone than older children.) A second activity could be to require the students to exert effort to keep their heart rate within a higher zone.

9. Have the students observe one another, being aware of the variety of activities necessary to maintain a heart rate within a specific zone. (Note: Although more fit children may require more effort to increase heart rate, this should not be a comparable measure of fitness. Have children pay attention to the reading on their monitor rather than attempting to imitate the workload of another student.)

Assessment

Ask for comments: What happened? Did some students reach their prescribed heart zone quickly while others had more difficulty? Why? You might want to repeat the activity, but this time have them set their audible alarms for the prescribed heart zone.

 Note: Some of the difference is because of differing fitness levels, but students' own Max HR also plays a part, so you might tell them they will learn more about this factor as the unit progresses.

Student Worksheets

The following worksheets correspond with the lessons in Unit II. The worksheets for this book have been designed as reproducible masters. Providing the students with a workbook of these worksheets will allow them to clearly record and monitor their progress.

Worksheet II.1   Using a Heart Rate Monitor

Name_____ **Date**_____ **Ambient HR**_____

A heart rate monitor is an electronic device that measures your individual heart rate continuously and displays it as a number of beats per minute.

What is the abbreviation commonly used for heart rate monitor?

The three parts of a heart rate monitor are:

     1.

     2.

     3.

Right now, my ambient heart rate is _____(A).

Right now, my ambient heart rate is _____(B).

What are the different function keys on a heart rate monitor?

     1.

     2.

     3.

     4.

Is it necessary to use a function key to see your heartbeat on the watch face? Yes or no.

(continued)

(Worksheet continued)

If yes, how is that accomplished?

Define *ambient* heart rate.

To find your average ambient heart rate:

A + B = C (total readings)

Average = (total readings) divided by (number of readings)

Find and record your average ambient heart rate (show your work).

My average ambient heart rate for today is _____.

From *Middle School Healthy Hearts in the Zone: A Heart Rate Monitoring Program for Lifelong Fitness* by Deve Swaim and Sally Edwards, 2002, Human Kinetics, Champaign, IL.

Worksheet II.2a   Pulse Rate—Heart Rate

Name_____ **Date**_____ **Ambient HR**_____

There are two basic methods of measuring anyone's heart rate: manually (with your hands) or mechanically (with some sort of a heart rate monitor). Your heart rate and your pulse rate are usually, but not necessarily, equal. "Heart rate" refers to the electrical impulses that cause your heart to beat, but "pulse rate" refers only to the movement of blood through your arteries. Take all readings in an ambient state unless told otherwise.

My *pulse rate* in three trials is:

1.

2.

3.

This compares to my *heart rate* using a heart rate monitor:

1.

2.

3.

Different locations in the body to take your pulse rate:

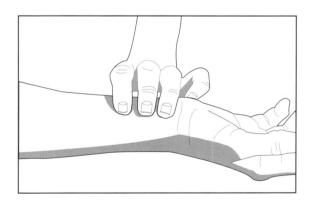 

What I learned:

From *Middle School Healthy Hearts in the Zone: A Heart Rate Monitoring Program for Lifelong Fitness* by Deve Swaim and Sally Edwards, 2002, Human Kinetics, Champaign, IL.

Worksheet II.2b   Resting Heart Rate

Name_____ **Date**_____ **Ambient HR**_____

Your resting heart rate is the number of beats in one minute when you are at complete, uninterrupted rest. It is taken in a prone position when you first wake up in the morning, before you lift your head off the pillow.

For five days, record your resting heart rate by counting your pulse before you get out of bed or sit up.

At your carotid artery, count your pulse for six seconds (using a clock with a second hand or digital) and multiply by 10 (add a zero to the six-second count) to get the number of beats per minute. Record that number each day in the boxes below.

1	2	3	4	5

When you have completed five recordings, add the five heart rate numbers together and divide by five (or number of days recorded) to find your average resting heat rate.

The total of my recorded heart rates is _____ beats.

Divide by the number of days = _____.

My average resting heart rate is _____ bpm.

What I learned:

From *Middle School Healthy Hearts in the Zone: A Heart Rate Monitoring Program for Lifelong Fitness* by Deve Swaim and Sally Edwards, 2002, Human Kinetics, Champaign, IL

Worksheet II.3a   Heart Diagram

Name_____ **Date**_____ **Ambient HR**_____

After watching *The Universe Within,* complete this worksheet by identifying the different components of the heart.

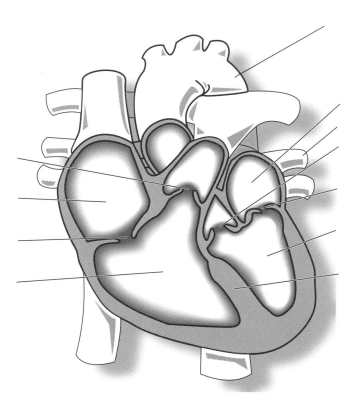

1. Aorta
2. Aortic valve
3. Left atrium
4. Left ventricle
5. Mitral valve
6. Pulmonary artery

7. Pulmonary valve
8. Right atrium
9. Right ventricle
10. Septum
11. Tricuspid valve

From *Middle School Healthy Hearts in the Zone: A Heart Rate Monitoring Program for Lifelong Fitness* by Deve Swaim and Sally Edwards, 2002, Human Kinetics, Champaign, IL.

Worksheet II.3b   Family Story

Name_____ **Date**_____ **Ambient HR**_____

Interview a family member or someone you know member about heart disease. Interview someone who has had a heart attack or open-heart surgery.

What could have prevented this?

What kinds of lifestyle changes occurred as a result?

From *Middle School Healthy Hearts in the Zone: A Heart Rate Monitoring Program for Lifelong Fitness* by Deve Swaim and Sally Edwards, 2002, Human Kinetics, Champaign, IL

Worksheet II.4   Delta Heart Rate

Name_____ **Date**_____ **Ambient HR**_____

Your delta heart rate (Δ HR) is a measure of your "heart rate response" to a change in body position. This delta heart rate test uses two positions: lying down and standing. Because you are unique—unlike anyone else in your class—it will be interesting to discover how you respond to this activity in comparison to others in your class.

1. With a partner, decide who will record first and who will do the activity. You will be monitoring for each other—the testing partner wears a chest strap and monitor, and the recording partner wears a monitor only.

2. The person doing the activity first puts on a chest strap and monitor, then lies down in a comfortable horizontal position. The recording partner puts on a wrist monitor and stands close enough (within three feet) to his partner to have his heart rate appear on the monitor.

3. The testing partner remains lying down for two minutes.

4. Review the heart rate for two minutes.

5. The recording partner should record the lowest number that shows on the monitor in the two-minute period.

6. The partner with the chest strap should stand up slowly.

7. The recording partner should observe the increase in heart rate to a high point, then be aware that it drops off.

8. The partner with the monitor should remain still (in a standing position) for two minutes. The recording partner watches the heart rate drop and records the heart rate after two minutes.

9. You now have these numbers:

      Heart rate *lying down* for two minutes: _____bpm (a)

      Heart rate after *standing* for two minutes: _____bpm (b)

(continued)

(Worksheet continued)

Graph the numbers by marking an asterisk (*) at the correct heart rate numbers on the "x" axis. Connect the points on the graph with a solid line.

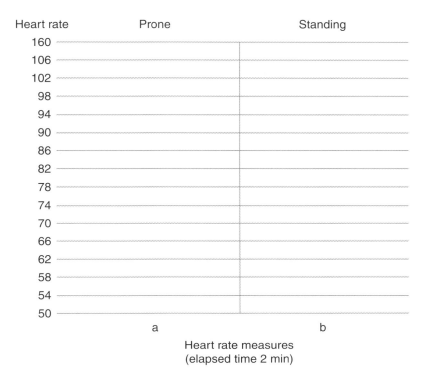

Calculate your delta heart rate, which is the difference between your standing and your prone heart rate numbers.

_____bpm – _____bpm = _____bpm

   (b)   (a)   =   delta heart rate

After both of you have completed the assignment and created graphs, compare them with one another. Did you respond the same way to the experience as your partner?

What might this tell you about your response to the physical challenge of your heart moving from one position to another? Why is there a difference?

From *Middle School Healthy Hearts in the Zone: A Heart Rate Monitoring Program for Lifelong Fitness* by Deve Swaim and Sally Edwards, 2002, Human Kinetics, Champaign, IL

Worksheet II.5 Setting a Heart Zone

Name_____ **Date**_____ **Ambient HR**_____

Exercising to develop a healthier heart can give you enormous health and fitness benefits. The benefits your body gets from exercise vary depending on the frequency, intensity, and time of the exercise experience. These effects range from a healthier heart to weight management to an increase in muscle endurance. Most people who attempt to train their body to high levels of health and fitness through exercise do so by using heart zones that keep the heart rate in a certain range for a specific period of time. A heart zone is a range of beats per minute, for example, from 120 to 140 beats per minute. In this activity we'll practice keeping our heart rate in a specific zone.

Define these terms as they relate to a heart zone:

Ceiling: _____.

Floor: _____.

To determine the heart zone you will work in today, find your ambient heart rate, add 20 bpm to it, and call that number the floor of your zone. Now add 20 bpm to the floor to establish the ceiling of your heart zone.

My ambient heart rate is _____bpm.

The *zone* I will keep my heart rate in for five minutes is _____ to _____.
                                                floor   ceiling

Doing this activity I observed:

From *Middle School Healthy Hearts in the Zone: A Heart Rate Monitoring Program for Lifelong Fitness* by Deve Swaim and Sally Edwards, 2002, Human Kinetics, Champaign, IL.

UNIT III

MANAGING HEART RATE

Unit Objective

In this module, students will explore the social, physical, mental, and emotional impacts on their health.

Unit Outline

The Influences

Biofeedback Monitor

Lesson Plans and Student Worksheets

The Influences

Heart rate is affected by any form of stress, including temperature, attitude, illness, fitness level, and diet. One of the important uses of a heart rate monitor (HRM) is our assessment; when we see our heart rate at elevated levels, it reminds us that we are under stress. This unit will explore the impact of physical, mental, and emotional stresses on the body and how to use a HRM for biofeedback.

Stress is an everyday fact of life. It's impossible to avoid. In fact, it's the human's most useful message that things need to change. Although we usually think of stress as being negative, it also can be positive. Too much to do, moving, job changes, and divorce are typically stressful and contribute to our belief that stress is always negative. But, positive life events such as falling in love, going to college, and getting a promotion also are stressful. We experience stress from our

- environment,
- body,
- thoughts,
- diet,
- feelings, and
- experiences.

Anytime the body is undergoing internal or external stress, it responds with an experience that we call the "fight or flight" response: when stimuli coming into the body are interpreted as threatening the regulating centers of the body, they give it information to speed up in preparation to confront or escape the threat. The pupils of your eye become larger so you can see better. Your muscles tense to meet the challenge. Your heart rate increases so that more oxygen and nutrients are transported to your brain cells and stimulate your thought response and your body can receive the chemicals it needs to respond to the threat.

If the body is not given relief from the chemical changes that occur during negative stress, chronic stress may result. This causes wear and tear on the body and a potential breakdown or compromise of the immune system. Too much total stress leads to a loss of concentration that can lead to accidents or overreactions that can play havoc with all areas of our lives and the lives of those we live with.

Chronic stress can lead to high blood pressure or hypertension, a disease that is unrecognized by at least half of the 25 million Americans believed to have it. Hypertension that is untreated can be deadly, resulting in heart disease, stroke, and chronic illness.

Another source of stress is our thoughts. How we interpret or label our experience and what we predict for our future can either relax us or stress us. If a student interprets a sour look from a teacher to mean that he is doing an inadequate job, it's likely to be very anxiety provoking. Perhaps that sour look has nothing to do with the child. However, an interpretation or perception of the gesture can be stressful because worrying produces tension in our body, which can ultimately escalate anxious thoughts and their results.

In some cases, the high blood pressure that many people experience is the result of an inability to deal with stress. The long-term effects of the racing heart and the chemicals released to deal with stress play havoc on the body. Sadly, most people become so used to stress that it becomes a background noise and is ignored. For others the negative stress is so bad that they lose themselves in self-defeating behaviors.

Biofeedback Monitor

You can't escape all the negative stresses of life or turn off your response. You can learn to manage your perception and habitual reaction to stress. The very centers of the brain that activate the physiological responses to fight or flight can deactivate them. People who use the information from an HRM learn this quickly. This valuable biofeedback tool gives us a minute-to-minute report of how the events of our day are affecting our heart. If you're wearing an HRM and a telephone call elevates the reading on your heart rate, you have an opportunity to step back and evaluate: "Why did this increase my heart rate and what can I do to change that?"

In a classroom, we are limited in the experiences we can use to show students how external factors affect their body. However, we can teach them about stress, encourage them to evaluate the stressors in their life, have them use a HRM to see how their heart responds to stress, and give them an opportunity to practice responding rather than reacting to these powerful environmental, body, and thought stresses. This results in proactive, not reactive, behavior.

The best thing we can do about negative stress is to know that it is a message that requires personal change. We can change the events that precipitate stress and we can remove ourselves from stressful situations that can lead to harmful outcomes from our over-stressed lifestyles.

The awareness of stress-causing episodes and positive response methods is an important tool for today's students. The primary focus here is noting the physiological changes that occur with stress and using visualization or "mindful recovery," with the feedback from the HRM data, as a coping practice. We then will address the positive stressors involved in exercise and recovery.

Lesson Plans

The following lessons and activities deal with helping students recognize the relationship between their heart rates and the stresses in their lives.

Lesson III.1   What Is Stress?

Stress is our body's response to the demands of life stresses. Stressors can be emotional, social, physical, or environmental demands.

Background provided to your students should include an explanation and a facilitated discussion about the kinds of stresses that can occur in our lives. Under stress, a number of physical changes occur in the body. One of the easiest changes to identify is a change in heart rate, which in most people becomes elevated during a stressful occurrence and lowered when the stress is removed.

Emphasis should be placed on making students aware that some stresses are short-lived—such as being late for class or worrying about a forthcoming exam—while others are prolonged, such as a chronic illness or a divorce in the family. Additionally, the students should know that several small stresses that by themselves may seem relatively insignificant can add up to have a large impact. Stress is cumulative. For example, over-sleeping, unironed clothes, a missing hairbrush, being late for the bus, and leaving your homework at home. If these all happened on different days, it's not significant, but if they all happened this morning—overwhelming!

Outcome

- Students will identify some stressors in their lives and explore healthful ways to respond.

Materials

- HRM
- Student journals
- "What Is Stress?" worksheet on pages 47-48

Activity

1. Hand out the "What Is Stress?" worksheet. As a class, discuss the word "stress." How do students hear it used and what does it refer to?

2. Put on monitors and get heat rate readout. Record ambient heart rate.

3. Ask for some examples of stress that they are familiar with. Some examples might be associated with decision making, assignments, expectations of others or themselves, changed plans, loss or death, and so forth.

4. Using the "What Is Stress?" worksheet, have students list five times in the past week that they experienced stress.

5. After they make their list, have them try to remember the way their body reacted to the stress (e.g., heart racing, sweating, muscles tightening).

6. Now have them note their heart rate numbers. Then tell them to visualize one of their stressful events and have them monitor their heart rate. How did it respond?

7. Have students work with a partner to come up with a list of ways they could deal with stress. What are some positive and negative coping methods? Did they use any of these methods to cope with their episodes?

8. Talk about using visualization to slow heart rate, calm breathing, and relax. Have students finish the worksheet and ask for volunteers to share their visualization statements.

Assessment

Have the students create a self-help stress poster. On one half of the poster they include drawings, pictures, words, and other things that relate to stressors in their life. On the other half have them describe positive sights, sounds, thoughts, and actions that help them cope with stress. Share as a class and post.

Extension

Current research is showing an impact on physical response to various "scents." Explore the impact of herbal smells such as lavender, lemon, and thyme on heart rate and make some observed assumptions about our senses and response.

Lesson III.2   Identifying Stressors

Screening to recognize what causes our stress is the first step in learning how to deal with stress appropriately.

Outcome

Students will be able to recognize and identify some stressors in their life.

Materials

- HRM
- "Coping With Stress" worksheet on page 49

Activity

1. Have the students put on a HRM and get in groups of four or five.

2. Have them each record their ambient heart rate and ask them to continue to monitor their ambient heart rate every two minutes during this activity.

3. Have them assign one member of the group to note the time. Tell the students when to record their heart rate and to make a note at each time check about what is going on in the group at that time.

4. Then tell them that their task is to brainstorm all the stressful things they can think of in the next 10 minutes. Remind them to think in multiple areas of health: physical, mental, social, and environmental.

5. Tell students to report on the items that they came up with as a group. As a class, make a list of these on the board.

6. Here is a list of some stressful events they may not think of, which you can help them add to the class list as the reports are given:

    The death of a friend or family member

    The divorce of parents

    The marriage of a parent

    A new family member through marriage or birth

    Peer pressure

    Grades

    Dating or beginning to date

    Suspension from school

    A serious illness in the family

    Moving

    Sports

    Clubs

    A job or loss of a job

    Parental arguments

Being new in school

Having an outstanding personal achievement

Hospitalization of a family member

A parent changing jobs

A lot of time alone

An older sibling leaving home

7. Each group must add five new items to the current list; they cannot restate a stress that another group already has identified. If you prefer, you can assign them roles for cooperative learning groups with a recorder, reporter, or facilitator.

8. Next, as a class, discuss what they saw happen with their ambient heart rate. Some will see that there were marked increases in their heart rate when they were discussing issues that were personally stressful. Tell them that periods of high stress can result in illness and that their heart rate should be seen as a signal that they should take steps to reduce the stress in their life.

9. Next, discuss the different responses we make to stress and then label them positive or negative.

10. Have the students complete the "Coping With Stress" worksheet.

11. Review this lesson in two weeks.

Assessment

Assess the completion of the worksheet and students' response to the awareness raising.

Lesson III.3   Recovery Heart Rate

The recovery heart rate is a measure of how quickly your heart returns to prestress levels. In this lesson we will focus on the recovery of the heart after the stress of physical exercise. In general, people with a higher level of fitness have a faster drop in their heart rate from the effort of exercise than people who are not fit. When fitness professionals are assessing recovery heart rate, the recovery rate typically is measured for one to two minutes after the end of the exertion.

The complete recovery heart rate is the time between the moment you stop exercising and the time your heart rate returns to the pre-exercise level. The complete recovery heart rate may require as long as an hour after the end of the exertion.

In addition to the role played by becoming more fit, we can use "mindful recovery" to improve, to some extent, the rate at which the body recovers from the stress of exertion. In other words, we can use mental biofeedback to consciously regulate our recovery rate. Mindful recovery is an excellent skill to develop to deal with stressful situations.

Mindful recovery involves visualization, deep (abdominal) breathing, comfortable body positioning, and the use of other relaxation techniques to purposefully lower your heart rate as rapidly as possible. With practice, students can develop their own coping strategies for managing their heart rate and their stress level in a variety of situations.

Outcome

Students will calculate their recovery heart rate.

Materials

- HRM
- "Recovery Heart Rate" worksheet on pages 50-51

Activity

1. Have the students record their ambient heart rate on their worksheet. Tell them they are going to see how their heart responds to activity and to rest that occurs immediately after activity. There are two types of rest: complete and active. Use complete rest or complete cessation of movement for this activity.

2. Have students put on monitors and ensure they can get a reading of their heart rate.

3. Instruct or lead students in an aerobic activity that raises their heart rate 30 to 50 beats above their ambient heart rate for five minutes. Examples of classroom aerobic activity might be jumping in place or using a chair to move rapidly (every 30 seconds) from a standing position to a sitting one.

4. Record the peak heart rate.

5. Now that the students are familiar with the process, repeat the activity again. At the end of the five minutes of activity, after the students have made note of their exercise heart rate, ask them to begin a mindful recovery by sitting quietly or lying down with their eyes closed. Encourage them to breathe deeply. Give them specific instruction that you want them to lower their heart rate. Encourage them to focus on mindful recovery.

6. After two minutes, have students record their heart rate again.

7. Instruct the students to subtract their two-minute post-exercise heart rate from the heart rate they recorded at the end of the five-minute exercise period. The difference is their recovery heart rate.

8. Explain to students that they have experienced a recovery heart rate. Have them fill in the question on their worksheet.

9. Record the ambient heart rate again.

10. If time permits, repeat the process and have them compare their results to the first experience.

 Since students' ability to measure recovery heart rate should improve with practice, this skill should be repeated often enough that they can do a recovery heart rate with little explanation. Each student will benefit from the awareness of the "relaxing" techniques that work best for them. You may consider trying some additional stimuli to aid relaxation such as music or dimmed lights. Have the students draw comparisons of these different settings for themselves.

Assessment

After the students have completed their worksheets, have them make a list of the strategies they used to lower their heart rate. Ask them how they would adjust their recovery process in the future. Give them additional opportunities to practice this skill. (Using meditative music is useful in this activity.)

Lesson III.4   Stress Response

Stress is universal—everyone experiences it every day. We're all exposed to environmental stress such as overcrowding, noise pollution, and grass seed pollen. Any change that forces you to change or adapt can produce stress.

Perception is a common source of stress. We encounter a situation that appears threatening and we activate the fight or flight response.

Not all stress is bad. The stress response helps mobilize us in times of danger and motivates us to try new things. The level of "healthful" stress varies by individual. We need to develop the coping skills to maintain a healthy response to the level of stress in our life.

Outcome

- Students will design and implement an action plan for dealing with stress.

Materials

- HRM
- Student journals
- "Stress Response" worksheet on page 52

Activity

1. Have the students do a delta heart rate measure as a warm-up.
2. Review the areas they identified as stress causing and their coping methods from their "What Is Stress?" worksheet.
3. Tell the students they are going to apply the information they have learned about identifying their stressors to creating an action plan for dealing effectively with stress.
4. Go over the "Stress Response" worksheet, and then tell students to use the information they have on previous worksheets to design an action plan.
5. Set criteria for checking their progress on the action plan.

Assessment

Using coping statements, have students write a poem for helping themselves cope with stress and then use it to design a greeting card. Criteria could include the length of the verse, the format, and the number of coping mechanisms, and it could cover the four response areas.

Lesson III.5   Diet and Heart Rate

Your heart rate is controlled involuntarily, with normal resting heart rates ranging from 50 to 80 beats per minute (bpm). However, in highly trained athletes, resting heart rates in the low 30-bpm range are common, and they are taxed to the maximum in strenuous exercise. According to Dave Martin, PhD, rates as high as 210 to 230 bpm have been recorded.

If left alone, your heart regulates its own rate automatically, but there are a number of factors that can change the rate of your heart's contractions.

You can integrate this lesson with home economics and social studies.

Outcome

Students will recognize the change in their heart rate from the consumption of various foods.

Materials

- HRM
- A variety of snack foods
- "Diet and Heart Rate" worksheet on pages 53-54

 Each group should have the same variety of snack foods, with at least one sample for each student in the group to try.

Activity

Note that this activity is best done with two monitors per group to avoid false readings from cross talk, which sometimes occur when the receivers are too close to one another. Students should recognize that once their heart rate is elevated due to food, it won't recover during the class period. Therefore, each student does only one measurement.

1. Break the class into small groups of four to six and have them work with a partner.

2. Make lists (as a group) of common foods that the students would expect to increase their heart rate.

3. Share as a class and have each group give justification for its choices (e.g., the idea that spicy or hot foods such as salsa increase body temperature—this is called thermogenesis).

4. In partners, have the students determine who will go first—student A—and who will go second—student B.

5. Each student A in turn wears the HRM and records her ambient heart rate and then consumes a portion of one of the food samples. At one-minute intervals, her partner records the heart rate. After 15 recordings have been made, change the monitor to student B and repeat the process.

6. After the group is finished, have the students create a graph of their recordings.

7. Regroup students into groups according to the food they tried. Have them make a new graph using all data.

Assessment

Have the students analyze the data they observed and write a short paper about it: What happened? Were there different responses to the same food? What could cause this? How will they use this knowledge in planning their diet?

 Show the overhead of the predominance of disease based on dietary trends.

Multicultural Extension

Have students look at other cultures: What dietary factors may influence heart rate? As an extension exercise, let students explore various cultures' dietary factors.

 You can group the samples and recordings by carbohydrates, fats, and protein.

Student Worksheets

The following worksheets correspond with the lessons in Unit III.

Worksheet III.1   What Is Stress?

Name_____ **Date**_____ **Ambient HR**_____

Stress is:

In the past week, five episodes of stress I experienced were:

    1.

    2.

    3.

    4.

    5.

Was the stressor in each case emotional/social or physical/environmental?

    1.

    2.

    3.

    4.

    5.

(continued)

(Worksheet continued)

Some of my physical responses to stress are:

As I visualized a stressful event, my heart rate change in one minute was:

_____bpm to _____bpm

* If there was no change in heart rate numbers, what might it mean?

Some methods for coping with stress are:

Positive   Negative

Using these coping methods, design a visualization that would help you to relax. Be sure to use descriptors that involve your senses:

From *Middle School Healthy Hearts in the Zone: A Heart Rate Monitoring Program for Lifelong Fitness* by Deve Swaim and Sally Edwards, 2002, Human Kinetics, Champaign, IL.

Worksheet III.2   Coping With Stress

Name_____ **Date**_____ **Ambient HR**_____

I am aware that even when I cannot change the stresses in my life, I have the personal power to change how I behave when these events occur. When I react without thinking it is called a "reaction." When I take charge of my reaction to stress it is called a "response."

Stressors in my life that I am personally unable to change include:

1.

2.

3.

The first event I will focus on practicing response vs. reaction is:

This is how I will make this change:

Explain what you have learned about the difference between reacting to a stressor vs. responding to a stressor:

After two weeks, this is what I have learned from my effort to respond rather than react to the stressors in my life:

From *Middle School Healthy Hearts in the Zone: A Heart Rate Monitoring Program for Lifelong Fitness* by Deve Swaim and Sally Edwards, 2002, Human Kinetics, Champaign, IL.

Worksheet III.3   Recovery Heart Rate

Name_____ **Date**_____ **Ambient HR**_____

Write a definition of "recovery heart rate":

Write a definition of "mindful recovery":

Since recovery heart rate is a measure of how quickly your heart rate recovers after physical exertion, you will be asked to stress your body with physical activity until your heart rate is at least 30 to 50 beats above the ambient heart rate you recorded above. Maintain that activity level for five minutes. Record the highest number ("peak heart rate") that you see on your heart rate monitor during the activity time.

After the activity phase you will begin mindful recovery and record your heart rate again in two minutes. You may choose any process you want to lower your heart rate. Some people like to lie down, close their eyes, breathe deeply, or elevate their feet. You may want to try different ways to find the most effective one for you.

    A. My peak heart rate during the five minutes of activity is _____ bpm.

    B. My heart rate after two minutes of rest is _____ bpm.

    C. My recovery heart rate is (A minus B) _____ bpm.

What do you expect to see in your recovery heart rate as your heart becomes fitter and/or you become more skilled at mindful recovery?

Explain why:

Now repeat the same activity; this time use chart III.1 to track your heart rate activity. Were the two trial results the same? If not, what do you think accounts for the difference?

(continued)

(Worksheet continued)

The following chart indicates my recovery heart rate response:

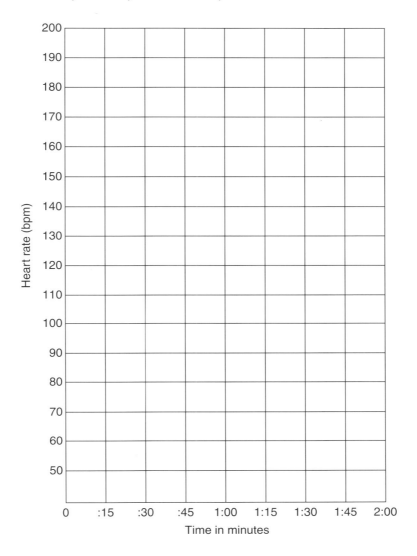

From *Middle School Healthy Hearts in the Zone: A Heart Rate Monitoring Program for Lifelong Fitness* by Deve Swaim and Sally Edwards, 2002, Human Kinetics, Champaign, IL.

Worksheet III.4   Stress Response

Name_____ **Date**_____ **Ambient HR**_____

I am aware that I have the personal power to change my life to decrease the stressful events I will encounter.

Stressors in my life I can work to change include:

    1.

    2.

    3.

The first event I will focus on changing is _____.

Anytime I make a change, there are factors that will support making the change and factors that will deter me from making the change. If they are identified in advance I can look for the supporters and avoid the saboteurs.

    Positive support   Negative detractors

My plan of action, I will:

    1.

    2.

    3.

After two weeks, this is what I have learned from this attempt to manage stressors in my life:

From *Middle School Healthy Hearts in the Zone: A Heart Rate Monitoring Program for Lifelong Fitness* by Deve Swaim and Sally Edwards, 2002, Human Kinetics, Champaign, IL.

Worksheet III.5   Diet and Heart Rate

Name_____ **Date**_____ **Ambient HR**_____

The foods our group sampled were:

     1.

     2.

     3.

     4.

     5.

     6.

I predict that heart rate will/will not be affected. Why?

The food I sampled _____.

(continued)

The following chart indicates my heart rate response to the food sample:

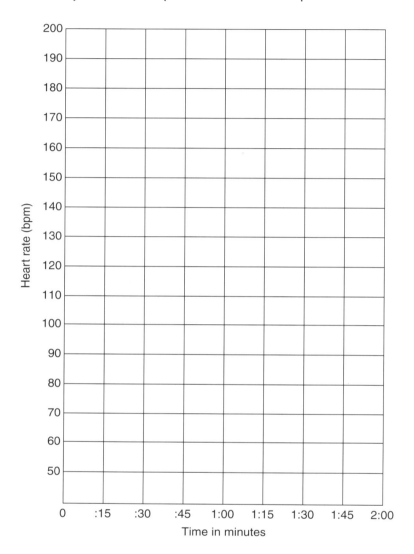

Reflections:

From *Middle School Healthy Hearts in the Zone: A Heart Rate Monitoring Program for Lifelong Fitness* by Deve Swaim and Sally Edwards, 2002, Human Kinetics, Champaign, IL.

UNIT IV

DESIGNING A HEART ZONE TRAINING PLAN

Unit Objective

Goal setting is an important life skill. In this module we will review the importance of the goal-setting process, learn some additional measures to help students set goals, create a plan that uses information already learned in the curriculum, and create an individual Heart Zone Training (HZT) plan unique to the student.

Unit Outline

Goal Setting: Lifelong Fitness

Heart Zone Training

Determining Maximum Heart Rate

Submaximum Heart Rate

Lesson Plans and Student Worksheets

Goal Setting: Lifelong Fitness

There are three variables in an exercise program that can be used to individualize a workout. They are

- *frequency* (F), or how often you exercise;
- *intensity* (I), or how hard you exercise; and
- *time* (T), or how long you exercise.

A useful acronym, using the first letter of each of these variables, has been developed to help students understand these important fitness components. The acronym is FIT.

According to the latest 1996 Surgeon General's Report on Physical Activity, "people of all ages can improve the quality of their lives through a lifelong practice of moderate physical activity." Lifelong fitness is, indeed, the goal of the principles of this curriculum. However, our goal is to help the student understand that for most people there is a direct relationship between the level of fitness attained and the health of the individual. People who are already active can enhance their fitness by changing the variables in the FIT acronym. People who are not fit can use the principles of the acronym to get started.

The goal of the Surgeon General's Report is physical activity of any type. Its goal is to increase the movement for the de-conditioned or unfit person. The report focuses on frequency and time, not intensity, and it may misrepresent fitness concepts by leading people to believe that very little effort (which is better than no effort) is as good as more intense effort. In many ways this makes sense because most people who avoid exercise have the belief that the longtime saying, "no pain, no gain" is still true. They may have memories of physical education teachers who punished them for lack of interest or performance by asking them to engage in push-ups, run around the track, or participate in activities that were painful. Using exercise as a punishment will never help physical education programs—it sends the wrong message to all. In addition, fitness professionals have been eager to focus less on intensity because one of the risks for exercise injury is the intensity of the activity. Moreover, people who quit fitness programs are often those who push themselves too hard, too long, or too often. They overtrain. It's much easier to get new exercisers to stick with a program when they exercise at an appropriate level of intensity. Then when they get hooked, they may increase frequency, intensity, and time on their own individual plan. A person can

- exercise more frequently at a lower intensity and for a shorter period of time,
- exercise more intensely less often for a shorter period of time, or
- exercise for a long time at a low intensity and less frequently.

The current research reveals that if you want the benefits of exercise, it's the intensity that must be varied as much as the frequency or the amount of exercise time. Using heart zones to determine exercise intensity is one of the safest way to enjoy physical activity.

Exercise less intensely or in lower heart zones and you'll accrue the benefits of health. By adding intensity, there are metabolic changes in the muscles and all the systems of the body that result in fitness improvement. Add too much intensity and you may reach higher levels of fitness but there may be negative side effects: pain, injury, deconditioning, or compromise of the immune system. Ask any athlete how he gets through the pain of a high-intensity workout and he'll talk about going inside himself and blocking out the pain. He'll admit reaching a spiritual part of himself that transcends the physical experience and enables him to reach his goal.

The heart rate monitor (HRM) is the fitness hardware tool that provides the most accurate and easiest way to measure exercise intensity. This extraordinary technological tool with the ability to view the heart on a second-to-second basis allows the user not only to remain calm but to put out her best efforts to achieve her individual goals.

With the knowledge that exercising at different intensities gives us different benefits, many monitors now have a feature that allows the user to set alarms that notify her when she is moving in and out of various intensities or heart zones. The user, with awareness of how her body responds to the workload of her activity, can use these functions to set zones with ceilings and floors that allow her to realize the benefits that are being accrued at any given moment. An alarm sounds or visually flashes when the user moves above the ceiling or below the floor of these preset zones.

The user bears responsibility to exercise at a workload that enables her to stay "in the zone" during the exercise session. All of this is done within 99 percent of the accuracy of a medical electrocardiogram machine—the kind you see for cardiac monitoring in a medical lab, without the complexities or expense. This makes getting and keeping fit easier because you can "train" in less time and get more benefits.

In order to understand how heart zones work, the user will need to learn how to use the alarm and zone functions on the HRM. The changes that will occur as she manipulates the intensity factor in the FIT acronym will become obvious as the user reaches goals with more precision and efficiency.

There are a variety of HRM models, but they can be summarized in four major categories:

- *Continuous-read monitors.* These give you a heart rate readout only.
- *Zone monitors.* These allow you to program in one or more of your heart rate zones.
- *Memory monitors.* These allow you to store data from your workout and retrieve it later.
- *Downloadable monitors.* There are two types: (a) those that interface with a computer to "download" the data and (b) those that you can manually download.

Heart Zone Training

Sally Edwards, professional athlete and author of five books on cardiac monitoring, developed a successful method of training that has been the benchmark for a new way to look at the benefits of fitness. Edwards's heart zone concept is based on managing heart rate by first knowing how fast your heart can beat—measuring your maximum heart rate (Max HR).

Longtime users of HRM often praise this tool just as much for its ability to remind the wearer to stay emotionally calm as for the HRM's ability to motivate users to put forth their best fitness efforts!

A HRM measures relative stress not absolute stress. That is, it measures the current stress being experienced at the moment usually as a percentage of maximum heart rate.

If a HRM has an alarm function, it can be set to sound or flash when the user is above his ceiling or below the floor of his zone. If he works out too hard or too gently, the same alarm will alert him that he's out of the zone. It is the exerciser's responsibility to stay in the zone during his exercise session. In this way the educator is freed of the responsibility of monitoring an exercise that is at best "one size fits all." Students design their own individual programs based on their fitness goals, their current level of fitness, and their own maximum heart rate.

Since heart zones are based on a percentage of a user's maximum heart rate (the highest number of times one's heart can beat in one minute), our first task will be to determine the user's Max HR. There are a variety of methods for estimating Max HR and this unit will explore several. After your students have determined their Max HR, heart zones should be calculated. Next they can write some personal fitness goals and apply those to a workout program. This program should balance the time spent in each heart zone with the benefit derived from that heart zone.

There is no single training or target zone, no one range of heart rates, that is best for everyone. Each of our bodies is different and our fitness goals are different, so there are multiple zones, each with different benefits.

Each of the five heart zones is named for the benefits that are achieved when exercising within it. The more time spent in each heart zone, the more of that specific benefit you'll realize. For example, Table IV.1 shows us a few important things:

- There are multiple heart zones.
- Each of the heart zones is determined by 10 percent of your maximum heart rate.
- By working out in different zones, you receive different benefits.

Beginners will spend most of their exercise time in zones 1 and 2. Every workout will be in the lower three zones, because the first fitness goal is to improve the cardiovascular system—the heart and lungs—as overall stamina is improved. This results in achieving the key initial health benefits, as well as insuring safe exercise protocols for those who are not currently fit.

Table IV.1
The Benefits of the Five Heart Zones

Zone	Zone name	% Max HR	Benefit of zone
5	Red line	90–100%	Performance
4	Threshold	80–90%	Getting fittest
3	Aerobic	70–80%	Getting fit
2	Temperate	60–70%	Staying healthy
1	Healthy Heart	50–60%	Getting healthy

Determining Maximum Heart Rate

We have discussed the importance of maximum heart rate. The next step in the Heart Zone Training program is to determine, from the methods presented, each student's Max HR. This is a specific number—the maximum number of contractions per minute that your heart can make. There are some basic facts we know about Max HR:

- It is genetically determined.
- It is altitude sensitive.

- It is a fixed number, unless you become unfit (in adults).
- It cannot be increased with training.
- It is higher in women than in men.
- Drugs and medication affect it.
- Max HR that is high does not predict better athletic performance.
- Max HR that is low does not predict worse athletic performance.
- It has great variability among people the same age.
- For children it has been measured at more than 200 beats per minute (bpm).
- It cannot be accurately predicted by any mathematical formula.
- It can be test-day sensitive.
- Testing for it requires the person to be fully rested.
- Testing needs to be done multiple times to insure an exact number.
- It is sport specific.
- It is an individual's anchor to set their training heart zones.

Most exercise principles are based on pacing your workout in relation to your Max HR. Your Max HR is a measurement of the fastest that your heart rate can contract at peak exertion. Your Max HR is a fixed number (in adults) and a biomarker for the individual. Several long-term studies of fit individuals indicate that it is not related to age, as has been thought for so long.

For example, an active person at age 30 may have a Max HR that is between 150 to 210 bpm. If that person ages and simultaneously decreases her physical activity or gets sedentary, then her Max HR tends to decrease. Max HR in sedentary people, particularly as they age, does decrease. However, Dr. Dave Costill of Ball State University has done studies that follow the same fit individuals over a period of 25 years. This type of research is longitudinal rather than cross-sectional. Amazingly, longitudinal research on Max HR of individuals remains unchanged if they exercise at a moderate intensity regularly.

This fact can have wide-reaching implications in how we create exercise programs. Traditionally an older person who began exercising used an age-related formula to predict his Max HR and design his workout based on one training zone of 50 to 90 percent of his mathematical maximum, not his real Max HR. If, as we now believe, people who stay fit do not experience a decrease in their Max HR, we are training them to exercise with less intensity, thus predisposing them to be less fit and to further decline physiologically. The result is that we have an aging population who are training in the wrong zones and as a result are not getting the desired benefit.

Max HR is the anchor point to set individual heart training zones. There are two ways to assess Max HR: take a Max HR test to determine the true number or take several submaximum tests to estimate the Max HR fairly accurately. There are two ways that the students can determine their Max HR:

1. *Take a Max HR test.* This can be done if the individual administering the test is experienced with the protocol. This is an unlikely method for use in a class setting, but the test is fully explained in the reference book *The Heart Rate Monitor Guidebook* (Sally Edwards, 1997).

2. *Take a submaximum test to predict Max HR.* These tests will be described later in this chapter.

Max HR for children varies greatly among individuals. Few studies have been conducted on prepubescents, but the research shows that from the time in the womb fetal heart rates can reach well above 200 bpm while Max HR declines until full muscular maturity. Thereafter, Max HR appears to decline if the adult leads a sedentary lifestyle. If the individual exercises on a regular basis, particularly in zones 3 and 4, Max HR does not appear to decline, at least to the age of 50 years (the age of those individuals who currently are participating in longitudinal research).

For safety reasons, it is best to determine maximum heart rate by averaging a number of different calculations and determinations of Max HR. Submaximum tests—tests that are below the maximum—can be used to estimate Max HR. Following is the test protocol for Max HR to provide a knowledge base regarding these tests.

Maximum Heart Rate Test Protocol

The test is a continuous acceleration to reach Max HR in the two- to four-minute test time. Every 15 seconds, increase intensity such that the heart rate increases 5 bpm.

A Max HR test, such as the one described here, should only be performed after completing a maximal stress test and health appraisal by a physician.

Here is what's needed for the Max HR test:

- Runner testee with a chest transmitter
- Runner partner with a receiver watch and stopwatch
- 400-meter track and running gear or quality treadmill

Two- to Four-Minute Max HR Test

The two- to four-minute Max HR test can best be performed on a track and it requires a partner who can run with the student throughout the test, give heart rate readings, and set a hard pace. The runner being tested wears the chest transmitter belt while the partner wears the wrist monitor. Another option is to use a high-quality treadmill with adjustments for incline as well as speed. The following description is for the track; the process is the same for the treadmill but with a gradual increase of incline and/or speed every 15 seconds.

Start the test with an easy warm-up of at least five minutes or one to two laps. The goal during the warm-up is to get the student's heart rate to 140 bpm. After warming up, and without stopping, the student should gradually accelerate so that his heart rate climbs about five beats every 15 seconds. At the starting point, the partner sets a gradually increasing pace. The goal is to reach the maximum between two and four minutes.

At 15-second intervals, have the partners say the elapsed time and heart rate, such as "one minute, 155." Within a two- to four-minute window, if the pace is set correctly, the testee's heart rate will cease to climb even with increased effort and pace. Set that number as the Max HR and stop the test, cooling down appropriately. A diagram of your test might look like figure IV.1. If the runner reaches the three-minute mark, he can continue to accelerate but he should reach maximum heart rate in the next 60 seconds.

During that last 15 to 30 seconds of the test as the acceleration continues, partners keep saying the heart rate over and over. Eventually, the same number will be repeated because the heart rate won't go higher—it's a finite number. By the end, the runner is running extremely fast, no longer can talk, and is breathing rapidly and hard. Motivation is key to reaching maximum heart rate accurately.

Mathematical Formulas to Predict Max HR

There are three formulas used to predict Max HR: Ball State University Formula, Age-Adjusted Max HR Formula, and New Max HR Formula.

- Ball State University Formula

  Max HR for females = 209 − (0.7)(age)

  Max HR for males = 214 − (0.8)(age)

- Age-Adjusted Max HR Formula

  Max HR = 220 − age

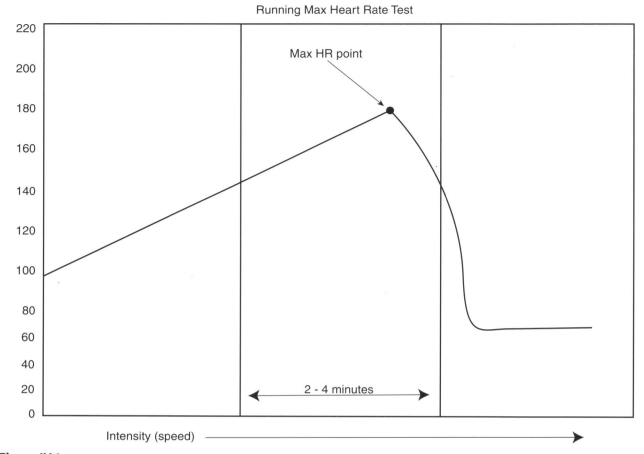

Figure IV.1

- New Max HR Formula

  Females: 210 − (0.5 × age) − (0.05 × your weight) + 0

  Males 210 − (0.5 × age) − (0.05 × your weight) + 4

Here's a sample calculation using the New Max HR Formula for a 100-pound female and a 150-pound male who are both 14:

Female: 210 − (0.5 × 14 years) − (0.05 × 100 pounds) = 210 − 7 − 5 = 198 bpm Max HR

Male: 210 − (0.5 × 14 years) − (0.05 × 150 pounds) + 4 = 210 − 7 − 8 − 4 = 199 bpm Max HR

Submaximum Heart Rate

The submaximum heart rate test is an assessment below your maximum heart rate to predict your Max HR. Following are four submaximum heart rate tests.

One-Mile Walking Test

Go to any school track (most are 400 meters or 440 yards around) and walk or stride as fast as you can in your current condition. Walk as fast as is comfortable. Walk four continuous laps.

The last lap is the important one. Use your HRM to determine your average heart rate for only the last lap. The first three laps are just to get you to reach a heart rate plateau and to stay there for the last lap.

Add to this average of the last-lap heart rate one of the following that best matches your current fitness level:

1. Poor shape: +40 bpm

2. Average shape: +50 bpm

3. Excellent shape: +60 bpm

4. Fit athletes: +70 bpm

This final number should be fairly close to your Max HR (e.g., an average 135 bpm last lap plus 50 bpm, for someone in average shape, would equal 185 bpm).

Highest Reading

The method most often used in a class situation is just to find the highest number you ever observe on your monitor when exercising hard and use that number as your maximum heart rate.

Step Test

Use an eight-inch step (almost any step in your school or home will do, even a sidewalk curb) and perform a three-minute step test. After you warm up, step up and down in a four-count sequence as follows: right foot up, left up, right down, left down. Each time you move a foot up or down, it counts as one step. Count "up, up, down, down" for one set, with 30 sets to a minute. It is important that you don't speed up the pace—keep it regular.

After two minutes, you'll need to monitor your heart rate for the last minute. The submaximum step test now can be used to predict your Max HR. Add to your last minute's heart rate average one of the following numbers:

1. Poor shape: +55 bpm

2. Average shape: +65 bpm

3. Excellent shape: +75 bpm

4. Fit athletes: +85 bpm

Your result should be pretty close to your Max HR (e.g., a last-minute heart rate average might be something like 120 bpm, to which 75 bpm is added, bringing the total to 195 bpm).

Chair Test

Use any open chair and sit-stand repetitively for 30 sits per minute, or one cycle every two seconds. At the end of one minute, take the highest heart rate you experienced and add 40 to 60 bpm to that number based on your current fitness level:

1. Poor shape: +40 bpm

2. Average shape: +50 bpm

3. Excellent shape: +60 bpm

4. Fit athletes: +70 bpm

Lesson Plans

Maximum heart rate serves as the anchor point for the HZT program. The following lessons will help students identify their Max HR and set zones based on that number.

Lesson IV.1   Step 1: Determining Maximum Heart Rate

There are many ways to determine maximum heart rate. For an athlete in high levels of competition, it is very important that this number be highly accurate. For our purposes here, we want the students to learn the skill process for determining Max HR. The number they get for application in this process will be an estimate, and depending on the method they use, the number may vary.

Outcome

Students will apply a variety of methods to determine Max HR.

Materials

- HRM
- "Step 1: What We Know About Maximum Heart Rate" worksheet on pages 70-71
- "Step 1: Submaximum Heart Rate Step Test" worksheet on page 72
- "Step 1: Submaximum Heart Rate One-Mile Test" worksheet on page 73
- "Step 1: Submaximum Heart Rate Chair Test" worksheet on page 74
- Calculators
- Eight-inch steps for half the class
- Journal page for each learner

Activity

1. Explain to the students that Max HR is the highest number of times their heart can contract in one minute, and that in this lesson they are going to learn some ways to find out what that number is.

2. Review the "What We Know About Maximum Heart Rates" worksheet with students. Tell them they will be using different measures to get their Max HR. The reason for a variety of measures is that, short of a true Max HR test, there is no one best way to determine it. This shows them different methods to use and helps familiarize them with the process. Ultimately they will average the results and use that number as their maximum. You will choose the combination of tests you want to use. We suggest first averaging multiple mathematical equations and using at least two of the submaximum tests to get a final average.

3. Have the students get partners and go to a step. Follow the instructions for the step test with one partner (A) testing and wearing the chest strap and the other partner (B) reading the monitor and recording the data. After student A has finished, repeat the process for student B.

4. Have the students record their data from the step test, one-mile test, the biggest number on their monitors, and chair test.

5. Now all students should have three or four "maximum" heart rate estimates. Have them find an average of the numbers and list that as their Max HR for class use.

Assessment

Have students define "maximum heart rate" and say why that knowledge is useful.

Lesson IV.2   Step 2: Calculating Heart Zones

Using Max HR as the set point, let's calculate zones.

Outcome

Students will design an exercise program based on their Max HR and the principles of heart zones.

Materials

- Heart Zone Training charts
- HRM
- Calculators
- "Step 2: Calculate Your Heart Zone Fitness Program" worksheet on page 75
- Journal page for each learner

Activity

1. Tell the students that now that they have an idea of their Max HR, they can calculate their five heart zones.

2. On the overhead, show them the following:

   In zone 5, the "Red line" zone is 90 to 100 percent Max HR.

   In zone 4, the "Threshold" zone is 80 to 90 percent Max HR.

   In zone 3, the "Aerobic" zone is 70 to 80 percent Max HR.

   In zone 2, the "Temperate" zone is 60 to 70 percent Max HR.

   In zone 1, the "Healthy Heart" zone is 50 to 60 percent Max HR.

3. Explain that each zone has a ceiling and a floor, and that these are the numbers the students will use to program their monitors later.

4. Have them calculate their zones and fill out the worksheet.

5. After they finish their worksheet, give them the Heart Zone Training chart on page 11. On the chart, have them find their Max HR at the top of the chart and circle or highlight that number. Now have them check their work against the chart and make any adjustments needed.

6. Have them program their zone 1 (Healthy Heart) on their monitor and set the ceiling and floor.

Assessment

Have students program their HRM with their zone 1, set the alarm, and be active to stay "in zone" for five minutes.

Lesson IV.3   Step 3: SMART Goals

Setting goals plays an important role in the success of any fitness plan. Goals should be both short- and long-term. They should meet the requirements of the acronym "SMART."

Outcome

- Students will apply the concept of "SMART" goal writing.

Materials

- HRM
- Overhead
- "Step 3: SMART Goals" worksheet on page 76
- "Step 3: Choosing Activities and Setting Goals" worksheet on page 77

Activity

1. Begin by asking the students what they think a "health goal" is and why a goal might be important. Let them brainstorm their ideas and list them on the blackboard.

2. Next, explain that they are going to learn a method for writing a health goal for themselves based on what they know about their current health.

3. Tell them these goals are called "SMART" goals:

    S = *Specific* means the goal states exactly what you mean.

    M = *Measurable* means you will know when you've completed or progressed.

    A = *Attainable* means you can accomplish it.

    R = *Realistic* means that it isn't filled with obstacles.

    T = *Timely* means it will "fit" into your life right now.

    Example of a student's SMART goal: "I will improve my recovery heart rate two-minute measure by increasing my walking distance one mile per week."

    S = She improves her recovery heart rate.

    M = She is working on the two-minute measure.

    A = She walks now and aerobic exercise is a way to improve her recovery heart rate.

    R = Adding one mile per week is a small percentage increase.

    T = She doesn't have any other after-school activity right now, so she has the time.

4. Write a health goal on the overhead and have the class determine if it is a SMART goal.

5. Now have them work on their own or in small groups to write two or three SMART health goals. They need to identify how it is specific, measurable, attainable, realistic, and timely.

6. Have a few share with the class.

You may want students to write one personal goal for each of the areas: social, emotional, and physical health.

Assessment

Have the students design health skits that demonstrate good health habits using the SMART goal theme.

Homework

Have students complete the "Choosing Activities and Setting Goals" worksheet.

Lesson IV.4   Step 4: Health Habit

Students who set goals and develop strategies and plans to accomplish those goals have more success than those who do not.

Outcome

- Students will synthesize what they know about their current health status into an action plan.

Materials

- "Step 4: Health Habit Action Plan" worksheet on page 78
- "Step 4: My Weekly Activity Time" worksheet on page 79
- Journals

Activity

1. Explain to the students that now they are going to apply the data they have recorded and the information they have about their wellness to design an action plan called a health habit.

2. Tell them to choose a goal about their health that is important to them and that applies the data they have about themselves. For example, maybe they learned that they can increase their lean mass with aerobic activity, and to do that they will join a city swim league that gives them access to the city pool after school each day.

3. Remind them about SMART goals and review the terms—specific, measurable, attainable, realistic, and less timely. Have the students focus their goals in one of the three broader wellness areas: health, fitness, or performance. The terms themselves accurately describe the building area and fit with the heart zones. Health-related goals can be addressed in zones 1, 2, and 3; fitness goals in zones 2, 3, and 4; and performance goals would focus training time in zones 3, 4, and 5. See figure IV.2.

4. Talk about support systems and ask students to name some supporters in their life. Explain to them that support can come from their mother picking them up from the pool after their practice or from a friend who wants to swim with them.

5. What are obstacles? Explain that sometimes an obstacle is as simple as that it isn't your normal pattern, not something you are used to doing.

6. Using their journal entries to remind them, have students design their health habit on the "Health Habit Action Plan" worksheet.

Assessment

Have the students design a chart that records their progress toward their goal.

Training tree

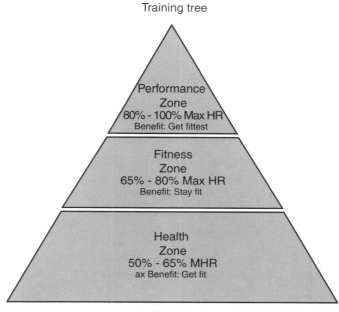

Resting
Below 50% Max HR

Use this tree to help you divide your workout time.
• Start by exercising all of your time in the Health Zone
• After this is comfortable, divide your exercise between health and fitness
• After this is comfortable, divide your time in proportion to your goal in all these areas

Figure IV.2   Training tree.

Lesson IV.5   Step 5: Fill Out Your 5-Step HZT Plan

Heart Zone Training is explained here in a simple five-step process.

Outcome

- Students will design their fitness program following the principles of Heart Zone Training.

Materials

- HZT charts
- "Step 5: Fill Out Your HZT Plan Fitness Program" worksheet on pages 80-81

Activity

We all know that we exercise more eagerly and for a longer duration when we are doing something we enjoy. The next step in creating a successful exercise program is to have the students choose activities they enjoy. Obviously, there are limitations on those choices. Because this is a school program, downhill skiing may or may not be an option. If it is the activity of choice and not an option during school, treat it as a weekend activity and spend class time on activities that can help develop the students' ability to perform better.

The basic components of fitness fall into five physiological areas:

- Muscular strength is the maximum amount of force exerted by a muscle or a group of muscles in a single effort. Muscular strength is generally improved by progressive resistance exercises in which the muscle or group of muscles must work against an increased resistance or weight. Isometric, isotonic, and isokinetic exercise would be used for improving muscular strength.

- Muscular endurance is the ability of a muscle or a group of muscles to sustain effort over a long period of time. Training for muscle endurance involves increasing the duration of an exercise by increasing the number or length of repetitions that the muscle performs.

- Flexibility is the range of motion of a specific joint and is generally specific to the joint being used. Flexibility is improved by static stretching involving a sustained effort extending the joint and lengthening the muscles for a specified amount of time.

- Cardiovascular endurance is the ability of the circulatory and respiratory systems to sustain strenuous activity for increasingly longer periods of time.

- Neuromuscular coordination includes those aspects of motor activities that enable a person to perform a physical activity or sport with efficiency of movement. This is called skill. The components are

    Balance—the ability to maintain neuromuscular control of a body position.

    Power—the ability to transfer energy into force at a fast rate of speed (explosive body movement). Placing resistance against the muscle group can develop power.

    Speed—the ability to move the entire body or body part rapidly. The improvement of speed depends on improved techniques and greater strength and endurance. Improvement is limited to the anatomical differences of the person, which is dictated by the overall body build.

    Agility—the ability to change the direction of the position of the body rapidly. Agility depends on elements of speed and power.

    Reaction time—the time elapsing between a stimulus and the body's reaction to the stimulus. Constant repetition of the stimulus can help to improve the reaction time.

    Kinesthetic sense—the ability of the individual to perceive the relationship of his body to the ground and space and make proper adjustments. Constant repetition and refinement can develop this aspect of skill.

Neuromuscular coordination can contribute to the other aspects of fitness by adding to the enjoyment of the activities that develop strength, endurance, and flexibility. Together they are important components of health-related fitness training.

Now that students have looked at their fitness level and diet and identified the activities they enjoy, they have all the background knowledge they need to design their individualized fitness program. Take the students through the five steps and let them fill out their program chart. The five steps to heart zone fitness are as follows:

    Step 1: Determine your Max HR.

    Step 2: Calculate your five zones.

    Step 3: Choose the activities you enjoy most.

    Step 4: Figure your weekly exercise time in minutes.

    Step 5: Fill out your HZT weekly planner.

Assessment

Have the students use their chart to write a SMART goal for their fitness program and then make a mobile of their goal and program steps that reinforces the concept.

Student Worksheets

The following worksheets correspond with the lessons in Unit IV.

Worksheet IV.1a   Step 1: What We Know About Maximum Heart Rates

Name_____ Date_____ Ambient HR_____

Facts about maximum heart rate:

- It is the highest number of beats your heart can contract in one minute.
- It is genetically determined—you're born with it.
- It is a fixed number for adults, unless they become unfit.
- It cannot be increased by training or conditioning.
- It is higher in females than in males.
- Drugs and medication affect it.
- A higher Max HR does not predict better athletic performance.
- It has great variability among people of the same age.
- For children it is commonly over 200 bpm but varies greatly.
- It cannot be accurately determined by any mathematical formula.
- It may vary from day to day because it is test-day sensitive.
- Testing it requires the person to be fully rested.
- Testing should be done multiple times to insure an accurate number.
- It is sport specific.
- It is the basis or anchor point used to set heart rate training zones.

There are three mathematical formulas for figuring your heart rate. Figure your heart rate using the three different methods.

- Ball State University Formula

    Max HR for a female = $209 - (0.7 \times age)$

    Max HR for a male = $209 - (0.8 \times age)$

My Max HR using this method is $209 - ($____ $\times$ ____$) = $ _____.

- Age-Adjusted Max HR Formula

    Max HR = $220 - age$

My Max HR using this method is $220 - $____ $ = $ _____.

- New Max HR Formula

    Max HR for a female = $210 - (0.5 \times age) - (0.05 \times weight) + 0$

    Max HR for a male = $210 - (0.5 \times age) - (0.05 \times weight) + 4$

(continued)

(Worksheet continued)

My Max HR using this method is 210 – (0.5 × _____) – (0.05 × _____) + _____ = _____.

My Max HR using the Ball State Formula: _____

My Max HR using the Age-Adjusted Formula: _____

My Max HR using the New Max HR Formula: _____

My average mathematical Max HR (subtotal divided by 3): _____

From *Middle School Healthy Hearts in the Zone: A Heart Rate Monitoring Program for Lifelong Fitness* by Deve Swaim and Sally Edwards, 2002, Human Kinetics, Champaign, IL.

Worksheet IV.1b   Step 1: Submaximum Heart Rate Step Test

Name_____ **Date**_____ **Ambient HR**_____

Maximum heart rate: the fastest your heart can beat in one minute, measured in beats per minute.

Use an eight-inch step (almost any step in your school or home will do) and perform a three-minute step test:

1. After you warm up, step up and down in a four-count sequence as follows: right foot up, left up, right down, left down. Each time you move a foot up or down, it counts as one step. Count "up, up, down, down" for one set, with 30 sets to a minute. It is important that you don't speed up the pace. Keep it regular.

2. Every 15 seconds have your partner record your heart rate.

3. You can predict your Max HR by adding to your last minute's average heart rate one of the following aerobic condition adjustments:

   Person in poor aerobic condition—add 55 bpm

   Person in average condition—add 65 bpm

   Person in excellent aerobic condition—add 75 bpm

Heart rate

0   :15   :30   :45   1:00   1:15   1:30   1:45   2:00   2:15   2:30   2:45   3:00

Time (15 sec intervals)

Last minute's average heart rate is _____ bpm.

Aerobic condition adjustment + _____.

My estimated Max HR step test result is _____ bpm.

From *Middle School Healthy Hearts in the Zone: A Heart Rate Monitoring Program for Lifelong Fitness* by Deve Swaim and Sally Edwards, 2002, Human Kinetics, Champaign, IL.

Worksheet IV.1c   Step 1: Submaximum Heart Rate One-Mile Test

Name_____ **Date**_____ **Ambient HR**_____

Maximum heart rate: the fastest your heart can beat in one minute, measured in beats per minute.

Go to any school track and walk four continuous laps as fast as is comfortable.

1. Determine your average heart rate for the last lap only.

2. You can predict your Max HR by adding to your last lap's heart rate average one of the following numbers:

   Person in poor aerobic condition—add 40 bpm

   Person in average condition—add 50 bpm

   Person in excellent aerobic condition—add 60 bpm

Last lap's average heart rate is _____ bpm.

Aerobic condition adjustment + _____.

My estimated Max HR one-mile test result is _____ bpm.

From *Middle School Healthy Hearts in the Zone: A Heart Rate Monitoring Program for Lifelong Fitness* by Deve Swaim and Sally Edwards, 2002, Human Kinetics, Champaign, IL.

Worksheet IV.1d   Step 1: Submaximum Heart Rate Chair Test

Name_____ **Date**_____ **Ambient HR**_____

Maximum heart rate: the fastest your heart can beat in one minute, measured in beats per minute.

Use any open chair at school or at home and perform the chair test.

1. Sit-stand repetitively for 30 sits per minute, or one sit-stand cycle every two seconds.
2. At the end of one minute, take the highest heart rate you experienced and add one of the following numbers:

   Person in poor aerobic condition—add 40 bpm

   Person in average condition—add 50 bpm

   Person in excellent aerobic condition—add 60 bpm

My highest heart rate at the end of one minute is _____ bpm.

Aerobic condition adjustment + _____.

My estimated Max HR chair test result is _____ bpm.

From *Middle School Healthy Hearts in the Zone: A Heart Rate Monitoring Program for Lifelong Fitness* by Deve Swaim and Sally Edwards, 2002, Human Kinetics, Champaign, IL.

Worksheet IV.2   Step2: Calculate Your Heart Zone Fitness Program

Name_____ **Date**_____ **Ambient HR**_____

Heart Zone	Number of beats per minute
100% Max HR	_____bpm
90% Max HR	_____bpm
80% Max HR	_____bpm
70% Max HR	_____bpm
60% Max HR	_____bpm
50% Max HR	_____bpm

Zone	Name	Heart Zone	Number of beats per minute
5	Redline	90–100% Max HR	_____ to _____ bpm
4	Threshold	80–90% Max HR	_____ to _____ bpm
3	Aerobic	70–80% Max HR	_____ to _____ bpm
2	Temperate	60–70% Max HR	_____ to _____ bpm
1	Healthy Heart	50–60% Max HR	_____ to _____ bpm

HEART ZONE TRAINING®

Training Zone (% maximum heart rate)	Fuel Burning	MAXIMUM HEART RATE														
		Max HR 150	Max HR 155	Max HR 160	Max HR 165	Max HR 170	Max HR 175	Max HR 180	Max HR 185	Max HR 190	Max HR 195	Max HR 200	Max HR 205	Max HR 210	Max HR 215	Max HR 220
Z5 RED LINE 90%-100%	GLYCOGEN BURNING	150↓135	155↓140	160↓144	165↓149	170↓153	175↓158	180↓162	185↓167	190↓171	195↓176	200↓180	205↓185	210↓189	215↓194	220↓198
Z4 THRESHOLD 80%-90%		135↓120	140↓124	144↓128	149↓132	153↓136	158↓140	162↓144	167↓148	171↓152	176↓156	180↓160	185↓164	189↓168	194↓172	198↓176
Z3 AEROBIC 70%-80%		120↓105	124↓109	128↓112	132↓116	136↓119	140↓123	144↓126	148↓130	152↓133	156↓137	160↓140	164↓144	168↓147	172↓151	176↓154
Z2 TEMPERATE 60%-70%		105↓90	109↓93	112↓96	116↓99	119↓102	123↓105	126↓108	130↓111	133↓114	137↓117	140↓120	144↓123	147↓126	151↓129	154↓132
Z1 HEALTHY HEART 50%-60%	FAT BURNING	90↓75	93↓78	96↓80	99↓83	102↓85	105↓88	108↓90	111↓93	114↓95	117↓98	120↓100	123↓103	126↓105	129↓108	132↓110

Reflections:

From *Middle School Healthy Hearts in the Zone: A Heart Rate Monitoring Program for Lifelong Fitness* by Deve Swaim and Sally Edwards, 2002, Human Kinetics, Champaign, IL.

Worksheet IV.3a   Step 3: SMART Goals

Name_____ Date_____ Ambient HR_____

   S = Specific means the goal states exactly what I mean.

   M = Measurable means I will know when I've completed or progressed.

   A = Attainable means I can accomplish it.

   R = Realistic means that it isn't filled with obstacles.

   T = Timely means it will "fit" in my life right now.

Example physical health goal: "I will improve my recovery heart rate two-minute measure by increasing my walking distance one mile per week."

   S = I will improve my recovery heart rate.

   M = I am working on improving the two-minute measure of my recovery heart rate.

   A = I walk now and aerobic exercise is a way to improve my recovery heart rate.

   R = Adding one mile per week is a small percentage increase.

   T = I don't have any other after-school activity right now, so I have at least 30 minutes per day for exercise.

My social health goal is:_____

   Specific =

   Measurable =

   Attainable =

   Realistic =

   Timely =

My emotional health goal is:_____

   Specific =

   Measurable =

   Attainable =

   Realistic =

   Timely =

My physical health goal is:_____

   Specific =

   Measurable =

   Attainable =

   Realistic =

   Timely =

From *Middle School Healthy Hearts in the Zone: A Heart Rate Monitoring Program for Lifelong Fitness* by Deve Swaim and Sally Edwards, 2002, Human Kinetics, Champaign, IL.

Worksheet IV.3b   Step 3: Choosing Activities and Setting Goals

Name_____ **Date**_____ **Ambient HR**_____

Choose the activities you enjoy most and set short- and long-term goals.

    Activities

    a.

    b.

    c.

Short-term goals (next three months)

Long-term goals (next 12 months)

Reflect on some of the ways this class can help you be successful in reaching your goals and on some of the obstacles you face in reaching your goals.

From *Middle School Healthy Hearts in the Zone: A Heart Rate Monitoring Program for Lifelong Fitness* by Deve Swaim and Sally Edwards, 2002, Human Kinetics, Champaign, IL.

Worksheet IV.4a   Step 4: Health Habit Action Plan

Name_____ **Date**_____ **Ambient HR**_____

I,_____,am ready to commit myself to the following action plan for three weeks.

My SMART fitness goal is:

     Specific =

     Measurable =

     Attainable =

     Realistic =

     Timely =

My supporters are:

I realize I can avoid completing my action plan by:

I plan to avoid doing this by:

In order to track my progress I will:

My reward to myself each day that I successfully fulfill the terms of my action plan will be:

Signed _____ **Witness/helper** _____

Review date _____

From *Middle School Healthy Hearts in the Zone: A Heart Rate Monitoring Program for Lifelong Fitness* by Deve Swaim and Sally Edwards, 2002, Human Kinetics, Champaign, IL.

78

Worksheet IV.4b Step 4: My Weekly Activity Time

Name______________________ **Date**____________ **Ambient HR**__________

My three favorite activities are:

1.

2.

3.

Fill in as much of the chart as you can with your planned workouts for the week. This corresponds with the HZT log page.

Date	Sport/ activity	Distance	Time	Time in zone					Workout benefit	Ambient HR	Rating	HZT points
				Z1	Z2	Z3	Z4	Z5				

As an example, the following chart is filled out.

Date	Sport/ activity	Distance	Time	Time in zone					Workout benefit	Ambient HR	Rating	HZT points
				Z1	Z2	Z3	Z4	Z5				
8/27	Walk	2 miles	20 min		10 min	10 min			Fitness	62	B	69
8/28	Swim	1500 meters	1:00	6 min	30 min	30 min			Performance	61	B	240
8/29	Bike	18 miles	1:15		9 min	41 min	25 min	6 min	Health	62	B+	271

From *Middle School Healthy Hearts in the Zone: A Heart Rate Monitoring Program for Lifelong Fitness* by Deve Swaim and Sally Edwards, 2002, Human Kinetics, Champaign, IL.

Worksheet IV.5   Step 5: Fill Out Your HZT Plan
Heart Zone Fitness Program

Name_____ Date_____ Ambient HR_____

Step 1: Determine your maximum heart rate.

      Estimated Max HR _____ bpm, or

      Tested Max HR_____ bpm

Step 2: Calculate your five zones using the Heart Zone Training chart.

Heart Zone	Number of beats per minute
100% Max HR	_____ bpm
90% Max HR	_____ bpm
80% Max HR	_____ bpm
70% Max HR	_____ bpm
60% Max HR	_____ bpm
50% Max HR	_____ bpm

Zone	Name	Heart Zone	Number of beats per minute
5	Redline	90–100% Max HR	_____ to _____ bpm
4	Threshold	80–90% Max HR	_____ to _____ bpm
3	Aerobic	70–80% Max HR	_____ to _____ bpm
2	Temperate	60–70% Max HR	_____ to _____ bpm
1	Healthy Heart	50–60% Max HR	_____ to _____ bpm

Step 3: Choose the activities you enjoy most.

    1.

    2.

    3.

(continued)

(Worksheet continued)

Step 4: Figure your weekly exercise time in minutes.

How many days per week? _____ days per week

How many minutes per day? _____ minutes per day

How many minutes per week? _____ minutes per week

Step 5: Fill out your HZT log page.

Complete the following statement:

This experience has …

HEART ZONE TRAINING WORKOUTS

Unit Objective

This chapter discusses a variety of workout lessons in both steady-state and interval styles. Each zone is represented; however, "Redline" workouts may not be appropriate for all students. As the students become proficient at these workouts, they can create their own. Have fun with it and stay in the zone!

Unit Outline

Training in the Heart Zones

Applying HZT Principles

Lesson Plans and Workouts

Training in the Heart Zones

Now that students have learned the Heart Zone Training (HZT) program and completed the five steps, they are ready to select workouts that fit with their personal goals and follow their individual HZT plans.

Workouts, exercise sessions, or training—whatever you call the time devoted to fitness—should have a purpose and a plan. The purpose might be to work toward improving endurance or strength or maybe to raise anaerobic threshold. A plan means that the time you spend doing this workout has a structure that includes warm-up, a main set, and cool-down.

All heart zone workouts are formatted the same way. Each includes a warm-up time, the actual activity time (or main set), and a cool-down period. These three parts to every workout are important components to use for avoiding injury and improving performance and should be followed in each workout.

Each of the heart zone workouts is coded with an icon to identify the difficulty or zone level it emphasizes. Because these icons appear on the workout sheets, students will be able to quickly and easily determine a workout intensity for the day.

Icon coding of the workout also matches the color-coding on the HZT wall chart available through the Heart Zones Web site (www.heartzones.com). The icon and color coding for identifying the level of challenge for each workout is as follows:

Red = Zone 5   Orange = Zone 4   Yellow = Zone 3   Green = Zone 2   Blue = Zone 1

Since many workouts are done in multiple zones, the zone in which the largest block of time is spent determines the chosen color and icon. We make recommendations about the zone level for each heart zone workout. However, as you work with the program you may adjust or add to the workouts so that they vary from the original code.

Before the workout section is begun, two important terms or concepts need to be explained: "interval" and "steady state."

Interval Heart Zone Workouts

"Interval" is the duration of a given intensity of training. That is, by varying the heart rate within a specific time period, you have completed one or more intervals. The interval training system has been supported by a tremendous amount of research to validate the premise that by raising and lowering your heart rate or stress and recovery cycle during a single workout, training benefits occur. This is called the "training response."

A class period does not allow for a lot of time to train, but we can still help students stay fit and work toward higher levels of fitness. Because of these time constraints, interval training of a high intensity can lead to huge fitness gains in short amounts of time.

Intervals add variety to training, and training benefits allow for an efficiently improved fitness level. Two of the benefits are

- increased endurance or aerobic capacity, which is measured by the amount of oxygen use ($\dot{V}O_2max$); and
- increased total number of calories burned with the increase of intensity.

There are four different types of intervals, defined by their duration: short or sprint intervals, middle-length intervals, long intervals, and endurance intervals. This is the most advanced use of the "time in zone" exercise plan. The four different interval types each affect different energy systems. Energy systems are the means by which the body transports and converts various fuels into energy. That's the primary point of doing intervals: to train the energy systems to use specific fuels and deliver nutrients to the muscles more efficiently.

Sprint and Middle Intervals Benefits

- Increased anaerobic enzyme activity
- Increased lactate tolerance (pH levels)
- Increased muscle strength in the specific muscles used:
- Increased power of fast-twitch muscle fibers (type II)
- Increased phosphagen use (adenosine triphosphate-phosphate creatine [ATP-PC])

Long and Endurance Intervals Benefits

- Increased anaerobic threshold heart rate
- Increased aerobic capacity.
- Increased lactate threshold
- Increased number of mitochondria (density of mitochondria):
- Increased oxygen transport profusion
- Increased amount of oxidative enzyme activity
- Increased fat metabolism

Another key to interval training is pinpointing the heart zone that matches a fitness goal. The five heart rate zones each can be subdivided into lower and upper zones, which narrows them from about 20 beats per zone to a more highly targeted 10 beats per zone—ideal for creating the precise effects desired in interval training.

There are four important pieces to interval-based workouts: how many sets of intervals, how much time for rest between intervals, the type of rest in between sets, and the work-to-rest ratio in each interval. Table V.1 illustrates the typical characteristics of the respective types of intervals.

Table V.1
Types of Intervals

Type of interval	Number of sets	How much rest	Type of rest	Work-to-rest ratio
Short	20–25	5 sec–1.5 min	Complete	1 : 3
Middle	8–10+	20 sec–2 min	Active	1 : 2
Long	6–10+	1 min–5 min	Active	1 : 1
Endurance	2–6+	2 min–10 min	Active	2 : 1

There are two types of rest: complete and active. After the work interval is over, there is a break or rest interval to allow time for the heart rate to drop to a lower zone. This is called a recovery period or recovery interval, and it allows the body to recover from the intensity of the interval, to shuttle away some lactic acid, and to resupply the muscles with fuel. Complete rest means that you slow to a near stop, while active rest means that you slow down but you continue to move: If you were running it would be a walk or a jog. If you were cycling, it means to shift down to lower gears and spin easily. If you were swimming, it means to continue to swim but to use a recovery stroke such as the backstroke.

In the beginning, a good goal could be one interval training session a week. Later, the student can add more time in the top two zones: Threshold (80 to 90 percent of maximum heart rate) and Redline (90 to 100 percent of maximum heart rate).

Here's an example: Let's say a student wants to do an interval workout day. He is a swimmer and usually likes to swim continuously for the amount of time he has, such as 20 minutes. To make it an interval workout, he takes that same amount of time, 20 minutes, and breaks it into five different parts. The first five minutes is a warm-up of mixed strokes. Then he starts two sets of five-minute intervals by increasing the intensity of his pace by about 5 to 10 beats per minute (bpm), with a three-minute active rest during the break between the two intervals. After completing the second of the two high-intensity intervals, he does a cool-down swim. If we were to diagram that workout, it would look like table V.2.

Table V.2
Long Interval Training Swimming Workout

	Activity	Time	Heart rate
HR = _____ % Max HR	Warm-up	5 min	60% Max HR
	Swim	5 min	85% Max HR
	Active rest	3 min	60% Max HR
	Swim	5 min	85% Max HR
	Cool-down	2 min	60% Max HR
Total		20 min	

Here are examples of interval workouts for three sports.

Swimming

Warm up with a mix of strokes for five minutes in zone 2—60 to 70 percent of maximum heart rate (Max HR). Start the interval session with two to four 50-yard repeats coming in at 90 percent of Max HR or zone 4. Rest after each repeat, until your heart rate recovers to 70 to 75 percent, the bottom of zone 3, before starting the next repeat.

Next, do two 100-yard repeats and drop the intensity by 5 percent. That is, come in at 85 percent of Max HR, zone 4, and depart at 75 percent, zone 3.

Finish the session with one 200-yard, steady-state swim at 80 percent (bottom of zone 4) of Max HR. Cool down the same as in the warm-up.

Cycling

Warm up for 10 minutes at 50 to 60 percent of your Max HR. Pick up the cadence and intensity to 85 percent of Max HR, and hold for four minutes, then drop back to 70 percent of Max HR for four minutes. Do this eight-minute repeat two to four times. Warm down by spinning at 60 percent of Max HR until you are home.

Running

Warm up at 50 to 60 percent of Max HR for at least 10 minutes. Next, increase the intensity up to 90 percent of Max HR and hold for one minute, before easing down to 60 percent of Max HR for two minutes. Repeat this four times and then warm down at 50 percent of Max HR. As this session becomes easier, add time to the work interval and keep the rest time as you transfer between a 1:2 to 2:1 to 2:2 ratio of work to rest.

 Interval training may be new to you. It gets you in great shape, fast. As a warning, too much high-intensity training may lead to lesser performance ability. Stay on the good side of HZT by balancing your interval training with steady-state training.

Steady-State Heart Rate Workouts

Steady-state exercise is that type in which intensity is kept constant throughout the duration of the workout period. This type of workout is different from interval training. During interval training, intensity or speed changes depending on the ratio of stress and recovery periods. During steady-state exercise, a speed or heart rate range is set and the individual stays at that intensity for the main body of the workout. Steady-state workouts improve cardiovascular endurance with the focus on a fixed heart rate for an extended period of time. Usually, these speeds or heart rate values are in the lower heart zones. This is common because in the lower heart zones—zones 1 to 3—it's possible to sustain longer workout times. This is due to the fact that lactic acid does not build up in the muscles and the blood, and the individual is not in an oxygen-compromised condition.

Steady-state training results in the exerciser building up certain cardiovascular abilities from the training experience that lead to improved fitness:

- Improvement in the aerobic enzymes necessary to improve oxygen consumption
- Improvement in recovery time between exercise bouts (intrarecovery) and between exercise periods (interrecovery)
- Improvement in the oxygen-carrying ability of the bloodstream
- Improvement in fat metabolism—the ability to burn fat as a primary fuel source
- Improvement in heart and lung function
- Increase in fat-free mass with a decrease in fat mass

An example of a steady-state workout for a swimmer is to swim at 65 to 75 percent of her maximum heart rate after the warm-up period for the duration of the workout. An example for a competent and fit swimmer doing a steady-state swim of 500 to 1,000 yards is shown in table V.3.

Table V.3
Steady State Heart Zone Training Swim Workout

Time	Intensity	Distance	Purpose
0–5 min	50–60% Max HR	< 400 yards	Warm-up
1 min	Complete rest		Recovery
10–25 min	65–75% Max HR	300 + yards	Steady-state training
1 min	Complete rest		Recovery
3–5 min	50–60% Max HR	< 300 yards	Cool-down

Steady-state training has so many positive features that it needs to be a standard in any fitness program. Workloads are at low to moderate exercise intensity so there's usually less strain, which equates with a lower risk of injury. Simultaneously there are huge fitness gains from this style of workout.

Applying Heart Zone Training Principles

A good starting point for a class might be to choose the students' workouts for the day, just as you would with a warm-up activity. Take them through a number of interval and steady-state options until they all understand the process. From that point on, they select according to their own personal goals—health, fitness, or performance.

You may want to create student workbooks for recording their plan and heart rate data and with log pages to track their workouts. If you want to add a point value to each workout, do so by multiplying the number of minutes exercising by the number of the zone in which it was performed. For example, 24 minutes in zone 3 would be 24 × 3 = 72 HZT points. As the students get familiar with HZT, have them set a point goal for the week or month.

Lesson Plans and Workouts

The following are a series of workouts. The first two are explained as lesson plans and student workout labs; the latter ones are simply in the form of student workout labs. Since all workouts follow the same basic format, once you and your students become familiar with the format it is not necessary to continue repeating it.

It would be a good idea to laminate the workout pages so they can be used over and over without reprinting.

Lesson V.1   Sustaining Zone 3 (Steady State)

The purpose of this workout is to burn a high percentage of fat as the source of calories as well as a high number of total calories. It's also good for students to hold their heart rate at a specific number and learn heart rate pacing without looking at their monitor. This inner perception of "how hard" or exercise intensity is a valuable skill to attain.

Outcome

- Students will note their training heart rate for zone 3 and apply that calculation to their workout.

Materials

- HZT log sheet
- HRM
- Sport equipment of choice
- "Sustaining Zone 3" workout on page 91
- Journal page

Activity

The basic format for all workouts is the same three parts: (1) the warm-up, (2) the main set of the workout, and (3) the cool-down. To "sustain" is to hold a steady heart rate. The assignment is to hold "at-about-around" the same heart rate number for the entire main-set time.

1. Have the students note their heart rate for zone 3 (70 to 80 percent of their Max HR).
2. Select a duration for their workout (e.g., 30 minutes, as we'll use here).
3. Explain that the warm-up is for 10 percent of the workout time, so they will stay in zone 1 for three minutes.
4. After the warm-up they will slowly increase their "work rate" until they are at 75 percent of their maximum, or the midpoint of zone 3.
5. Tell the students that they should feel challenged but will not be exercising too hard or too easy. It is a moderate intensity and can be taxing.
6. Have them spend 24 minutes in zone 3, at-about-around that 75 percent number of heartbeats.
7. They cool down for three minutes in zone 1.
8. Refer to table V.4. The "Aerobic" zone is so named because if you train there, you will get tremendous improvement in your ability to use oxygen, develop a stronger heart, get healthier lungs, and increase your muscle mass. There is a low chance of overtraining or sustaining an injury when training in zone 3.

Table V.4
Steady-State Workout

Step	Activity	Zone	Time in zone
1. Warm-up	Any gentle activity that stimulates an increase in blood flow	1	3 min
2. Main set	Sports activity of choice	3	24 min
3. Cool-down	Any gentle and slower activity, recovery level	1	3 min

You can allow the students to select the activity they enjoy most—skating, biking, walking, swimming, cardio exercise equipment, and so forth. Remember, enjoying exercise is a key to long-term exercise compliance.

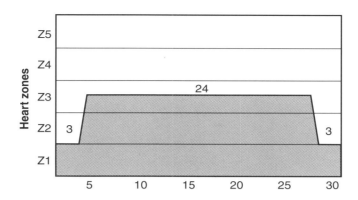

Assessment

Have the students write in their journal page regarding their impressions of this workout and the benefits they expect. Record their workout in their HZT log sheet.

Lesson V.2   Ricochet Workout

This HZT exercise uses all five zones. This workout can be adapted for running, cycling, swimming, race walking, skating, and snowshoeing. It is based on 400-yard sets that "ricochet" or are divided into parts. The first 1 × 400 yards in zone 2 is followed by 2 × 200 yards in zone 3, then 4 × 100 yards in zone 4 and an optional 8 × 50 yards in zone 5. Students recover to 50 percent of their activity-specific Max HR between repeats.

Outcome

- The students can experience a tour of the five heart zones.

Materials

- HZT log sheet
- HRM
- "Ricochet Workout" on page 93
- A track or other facility marked off in 400-, 200-, 100-, and 50-yard increments

Activity

1. Have students review their heart zones 1-5 from Worksheet IV.2, or use the HZT chart.

2. Check out HRM to students and have them program it for the ceiling of zone 2, with the alarms on.

3. Explain the format of the workout. (Running is the example used here to outline the progression, but again you can use any of the mentioned sport activities.)

4. Have the students warm up in zone 1 for at least 10 percent of their total time or training distance.

5. Have them run 400 yards one time with a heart rate in zone 2.

6. Students should have a recovery to the ceiling of zone 1 heart rate.

7. The second set is two repeats of 200 yards each in zone 3.

8. Tell them to recover to the ceiling of zone 1 heart rate.

9. The next set is four repeats of 100 yards in zone 4 with recovery to zone 1 between each repeat.

10. If you choose to have the students do a final interval in zone 5, they do eight 50-yard repeats at 90 percent (the floor of zone 5) of their Max HR. Again, they recover to the ceiling of zone 1 between

each 50-yard distance. This last set is called "red lining" and it's hard and fast, while recovery is long and slow.

11. The workout looks like table V.5.

Table V.5
Ricochet Workout

	HZT	% of Max HR	Estimated HZ points
1. Warm-up 100 yards	Z1	50% of Max HR	
2. 400 yards	Z2	60–70% of Max HR	
3. Recovery	Z1	50% of Max HR	
4. 200 yards	Z3	70–80% of Max HR	
5. Recovery	Z1	50% of Max HR	
6. 200 yards	Z3	70–80% of Mxa HR	
7. Recovery	Z1	50% of Max HR	
8. 100 yards	Z4	80–90% of Max HR	
9. Recovery	Z1	50% of Max HR	
10. 100 yards	Z4	80–90% of Max HR	
11. Recovery	Z1	50% of Max HR	
12. 100 yards	Z4	80–90% of Max HR	
13. Recovery	Z1	50% of Max HR	
14. 100 yards	Z4	80–90% of Max HR	
		Total HZ Points	_____

Optional

	HZT	% of Max HR	
15. 50 yards	Z5 floor	90% of Max HR	
16. Recovery	Z1	50% of Max HR	

For swimming activity, use only HRM with the feature/capacity rated for 20 feet below water surface.

Repeat the set if time allows, and students should always recover to the ceiling of zone 1 before starting another length in zone 5. For students to figure their HZT points, they will have to track their time spent on each interval.

Assessment

The benefits of this workout are those of multiple zones. By using this workout as a conditioning measure, you can assess the students' improved fitness levels by timing their recoveries. Have them total their HZT points and record them in their log.

Have the students regularly review their point goals for the week or month to help them stay challenged and positive towards their training.

Workout V.1   Sustaining Zone 3 Workout

The purpose of this workout is to burn a high percentage of fat as the source of calories as well as a high number of total calories. It's also good to hold your heart rate at a specific number and learn heart rate pacing without looking at your heart monitor. This inner perception of "how hard" or exercise intensity is a valuable skill to attain.

The basic format for all workouts is the same three parts: (1) the warm-up, (2) the main set of the workout, and (3) the cool-down. To "sustain" is to hold a steady heart rate number in beats per minute. The assignment is to hold at-about-around the same heart rate number for the entire main-set time.

Note your heart rate for zone 1 (50 to 60 percent of your Max HR):

　　　Z1 _____ to _____

Note your heart rate for zone 3 (70 to 80 percent of your Max HR):

　　　Z3 _____ to _____

The workout is for 30 minutes. The warm-up is for 10 percent of the workout time, so you will stay in zone 1 for three minutes. After the warm-up, you will slowly increase your "work rate" until you are at 75 percent of maximum, or at the midpoint of zone 3. You should feel challenged but will not be exercising too hard or too easy. It is a moderate intensity and can be taxing. Spend 24 minutes in zone 3 and cool down for three minutes in zone 1. A graph of the workout would look like the following:

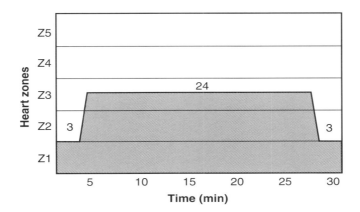

Step	Activity	Zone	% MHR	Time in zone
Warm-up	Any gentle activity that stimulates an increase in blood flow.	1	50–60	3 minutes
Main set	Begin sports activity.	3	70–80	24 minutes
Warm-down	Any gentle and slower activity, recovery level.	1	50–60	3 minutes

(continued)

(Worksheet continued)

Select an aerobic activity you enjoy—such as skating, biking, walking, swimming, or cardio exercise equipment. Remember, enjoying exercise is the key to long-term continuation. The "Aerobic" zone is so named because if you train there, you will get tremendous improvement in your ability to use oxygen, develop a stronger heart, get healthier lungs, and increase your muscle mass. There is a low chance of overtraining or injury when training in zone 3.

HZT point activity:

Z1_____ minutes $\times$ 1 = HZT points _____

Z2_____ minutes $\times$ 2 = HZT points _____

Z3_____ minutes $\times$ 3 = HZT points _____

Z4_____ minutes $\times$ 4 = HZT points _____

Z5_____ minutes $\times$ 5 = HZT points _____

Total HZT points_____

From *Middle School Healthy Hearts in the Zone: A Heart Rate Monitoring Program for Lifelong Fitness* by Deve Swaim and Sally Edwards, 2002, Human Kinetics, Champaign, IL.

Workout V.2   Ricochet Workout

This Heart Zone Training exercise uses all five heart zones and the recovery heart rate. You can adapt this workout for running, cycling, swimming, racewalking, skating, and snowshoeing. It is based on 400-yard sets that "ricochet" or are divided into parts. The first 1 × 400 yards in zone 2 is followed by 2 × 200 yards in zone 3, then 4 × 100 yards in zone 4 and an optional 8 × 50 yards in zone 5. Recover to the floor of zone 1 heart rate or about 50 percent of Max HR between repeats. This is called interval training.

Ricochet Workout

	HZ	% of Max HR	Estimated HZ points
1. Warm-up 100 yards	Z1	50% of Max HR	
2. 400 yards	Z2	60–70% of Max HR	
3. Recovery	Z1	50% of Max HR	
4. 200 yards	Z3	70–80% of Max HR	
5. Recovery	Z1	50% of Max HR	
6. 200 yards	Z3	70–80% of Max HR	
7. Recovery	Z1	50% of Max HR	
8. 100 yards	Z4	80–90% of Max HR	
9. Recovery	Z1	50% of Max HR	
10. 100 yards	Z4	80–90% of Max HR	
11. Recovery	Z1	50% of Max HR	
12. 100 yards	Z4	80–90% of Max HR	
13. Recovery	Z1	50% of Max HR	
14. 100 yards	Z4	80–90% of Max HR	
		Total HZ Points _____	

Optional

	HZ	% of Max HR	
15. 50 yards	Z5 floor	90% of Max HR	
16. Recovery	Z1	50% of Max HR	

Repeat the session as many times as your schedule allows, and always allow adequate recovery to zone 1 before starting another set. To figure your HZT points, you will have to estimate the time spent on each interval. Record your HZT points on your log page.

From *Middle School Healthy Hearts in the Zone: A Heart Rate Monitoring Program for Lifelong Fitness* by Deve Swaim and Sally Edwards, 2002, Human Kinetics, Champaign, IL.

Workout V.3   Cool Cycle Style Workout

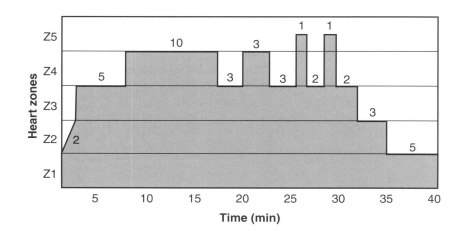

In this indoor cycling workout, the emphasis is to stay as relaxed as possible while moving through some tough intervals. Throughout this interval workout, focus on good climbing posture and strengthening the quadriceps and hamstrings. Stay "cool" by practicing relaxation techniques during the ride:

- One way is to hold the upper body directly over the pedal while changing hand positions.

- Slide back in the saddle for the seated climbs to develop more power and, as you stand, transfer your weight over the pedals from side to side, keeping the weight off the handlebars and using the power of your legs.

- Check your body position in a mirror to make sure your weight is not too far forward over the front wheel. Balance helps keep the body relaxed. This workout is all about staying relaxed while the body works hard.

This workout also can be performed on a stair-step machine.

 You can raise your front wheel off the ground three to five inches to simulate a climbing position if you want to make the workout "hotter."

Cool Cycle Workout Plan

Zone	Zone name	Time in zone	HZT points
5	Red line	2 min	10
4	Threshold	13 min	52
3	Aerobic	15 min	45
2	Temperate	5 min	10
1	Healthy Heart	5 min	5
Totals		**40 min**	**122**

From *Middle School Healthy Hearts in the Zone: A Heart Rate Monitoring Program for Lifelong Fitness* by Deve Swaim and Sally Edwards, 2002, Human Kinetics, Champaign, IL.

94

Workout V.4   Power Surge Workout

This is an interval workout that pushes your aerobic threshold. You will warm up comfortably in zone 2 for five minutes then rapidly increase intensity to raise your heart rate to zone 4. Stay in zone 4 for three minutes then recover to zone 1 for two minutes. Again, increase intensity, this time by 40 bpm to zone 5 and stay in the zone for three minutes. Recover to zone 1 for two minutes then repeat the entire workout.

1. Warm up for five minutes in zone 2 at 60 to 70 percent of Max HR.
2. Add 10 bpm for three minutes in zone 4 at 80 to 90 percent of Max HR.
3. Have a recovery period of two minutes in zone 1 at 55 percent of Max HR.
4. Add 40 bpm for three minutes in zone 5 at 90 to 100 percent of Max HR.
5. Have a recovery for two minutes in zone 1 at 55 percent of Max HR.
6. Repeat the entire workout.

The Power Surge Workout Plan

Zone	Zone name	Time in zone	HZT points
5	Redline	6 min	30
4	Threshold	6 min	24
3	Aerobic		
2	Temperate	10 min	20
1	Healthy Heart	8 min	8
Totals		**30 min**	**82**

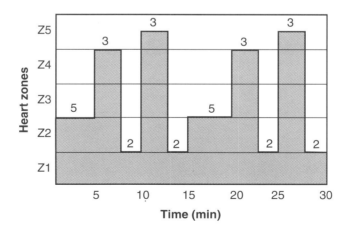

From *Middle School Healthy Hearts in the Zone: A Heart Rate Monitoring Program for Lifelong Fitness* by Deve Swaim and Sally Edwards, 2002, Human Kinetics, Champaign, IL.

Workout V.5
The Tourist

This 36-minute workout includes five intervals and touches four zones. Warm up in zone 2 for five minutes, increase to zone 3 for five minutes, then increase to zone 4 for two minutes.

The Tourist Workout Plan

Zone	Zone name	Time in zone	HZT points
5	Redline		
4	Threshold	5 min	24
3	Aerobic	15 min	45
2	Temperate	10 min	20
1	Healthy Heart	5 min	5
Totals		**35 min**	**94**

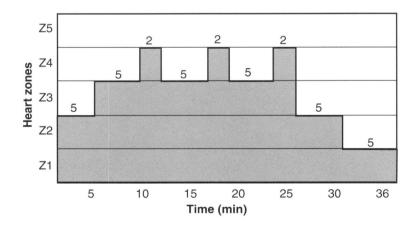

Step	Zone	Time in zone
Warm-up	2	5 min
Increase activity	3	5 min
Increase activity	4	2 min
Decrease activity	3	5 min
Increase activity	4	2 min
Decrease activity	3	5 min
Increase activity	4	2 min
Decrease activity	2	5 min
Cool-down	1	5 min

From *Middle School Healthy Hearts in the Zone: A Heart Rate Monitoring Program for Lifelong Fitness* by Deve Swaim and Sally Edwards, 2002, Human Kinetics, Champaign, IL.

Workout V.6   Five-by-Five Workout

This is a running workout. The purpose is to teach your running-specific metabolic systems to adapt to a constantly increasing workload every five minutes, which trains your cardiovascular capacity. This workout increases heart rate by 5 bpm, or a five-beat ladder, every five minutes. Subtract 20 beats from your Max HR to determine the top rung on your ladder and subtract 50 beats from your Max HR for your heart rate starting point on the first rung of the ladder. The range between these two numbers is your training zone for the "five-by-fiver." For example:

200 (Max HR) – 20 = 180 (ceiling, or top rung).

200 (Max HR) – 50 = 150 (floor, or starting rung).

Training zone for the workout is 150 to 180 bpm.

Warm up by gradually increasing from a walk to a slow jog to your starting-point heart rate. You should begin the main-set ladder by increasing your heart rate five beats every five minutes.

Zone	Minutes	Heart rate*	HZT points
1	0–5	Warm-up	5
3	5–10	150–155	15
3	10–15	155–160	15
4	15–20	160–165	20
4	20–25	165–170	20
4	25–30	170–175	20
4	30–35	175–180	20
1	35–40	Cool-down	5
Totals	**40**		**120**

*Example is for a student with a maximum heart rate of 200 bpm.

Five-by-Five Workout Plan

Zone	Zone name	Time in zone	HZT points
5	Redline		
4	Threshold	20 min	80
3	Aerobic	10 min	30
2	Temperate		
1	Healthy Heart	10 min	10
Totals		**40 min**	**120**

From *Middle School Healthy Hearts in the Zone: A Heart Rate Monitoring Program for Lifelong Fitness* by Deve Swaim and Sally Edwards, 2002, Human Kinetics, Champaign, IL.

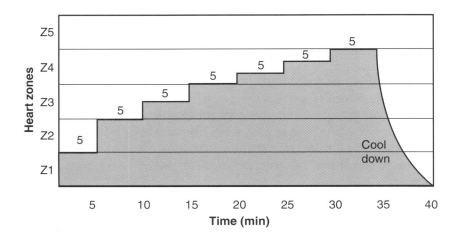

Expansion

Start by only going up the ladder. When you are in great shape, you should try going up twice in a single workout. The more times you go up and down the ladder, the more fit you will get.

Workout V.7
Tour of Zones

This workout lets you experience each of the heart zones. In the lower three heart zones—zones 1, 2, and 3—the training intensity goes from mild to moderate to strenuous. In the upper two performance zones—zones 4 and 5—the training intensity is very hard and hardest.

Start at 60 percent (zone 2) of your Max HR and hold that number as you complete a five-minute warm-up. Then, gradually increase your heart rate to 63 percent and hold that for two minutes before you increase it to 65 percent and then increase again to 68 percent. So every two minutes you will increase your heart rate 3 percent or 4 to 5 bpm. You should maintain that heart rate for two minutes and continue until you are at 90 percent of you Max HR. Then recover to zone 1. Before you begin, figure your heart rate for each phase of the workout. This workout is done in two-minute increments, increasing your heart rate every two minutes.

Tour of Zones Workout Plan

Time	Percentage	Sample if Max HR = 180 bpm
0–5 min	60%	108 bpm
5–7 min	63%	113 bpm
7–9 min	65%	117 bpm
9–11 min	68%	122 bpm
11–13 min	70%	127 bpm
13–15 min	73%	131 bpm
15–17 min	75%	135 bpm
17–19 min	78%	140 bpm
19–21 min	80%	144 bpm
21–23 min	83%	149 bpm
23–25 min	85%	153 bpm
25–27 min	88%	157 bpm
27–29 min	90%	161 bpm
29–35 min	60%	108 bpm, recovery

Review

In this short 35-minute workout, you have traveled through all five zones and experienced the intensity of the health (zones 1 to 3), the fitness (zones 2 to 4), and the performance (zones 3 to 5) zones that we call the wellness continuum. Each of these zones has a different feel and a challenge to it. The lower ones challenged you to remain quiet and peaceful and the higher ones required that you push yourself to reach near maximum. You should have found some heart rate zone numbers that you really enjoy and that you feel like you could train at for a long period of time. If you have, then you should return to them often.

(continued)

(Worksheet continued)

Summary of Tour of Zones

Zone	Zone name	Time in zone	HZT points
5	Redline	4 min	20
4	Threshold	6 min	24
3	Aerobic	8 min	24
2	Temperate	8 min	16
1	Healthy Heart	4 min	4
Totals		**35 min**	**93**

If we were to graph this workout, it would look like a long, low-rise flight of stairs.

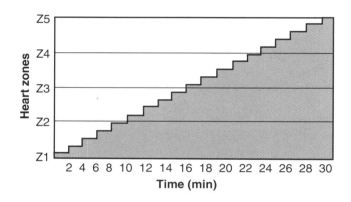

From *Middle School Healthy Hearts in the Zone: A Heart Rate Monitoring Program for Lifelong Fitness* by Deve Swaim and Sally Edwards, 2002, Human Kinetics, Champaign, IL.

Workout V.8   Footloose Workout

This is a zone 3 aerobic workout that makes a great cardio-conditioning workout. Warm up for 10 minutes at the ceiling of zone 1 and then increase your heart rate to zone 3 and maintain the zone for 30 minutes. This is called a steady-state training session.

Check your recovery heart rate on the cool-down. To test recovery heart rate, see how many beats per minute you drop in two minutes.

Summary of Footloose Workout

Zone	Zone name	Time in zone	HZT points
5	Redline		
4	Threshold		
3	Aerobic	30 min	90
2	Temperate	5 min	10
1	Healthy Heart	10 min	10
Totals		**45 min**	**110**

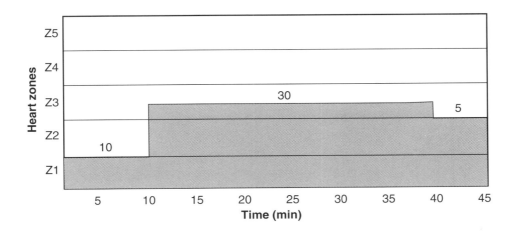

From *Middle School Healthy Hearts in the Zone: A Heart Rate Monitoring Program for Lifelong Fitness* by Deve Swaim and Sally Edwards, 2002, Human Kinetics, Champaign, IL.

Workout V.9　Threshold Workout

The purpose of this workout is to raise your anaerobic threshold heart rate (AT_{HR}) using long intervals in specific heart rate ranges. This workout can apply to almost any aerobic activity, but it is not for the beginner.

To do this 38-minute interval training session, you need to know your Max HR and your AT_{HR}. For your AT_{HR}, use the middle-point measure of your Threshold zone. For example, if your Threshold zone 4 (80 to 90 percent of Max HR) is 144–162, use the midpoint of the zone, or 153 bpm.

The workout involves four-minute segments at the midpoint of zone 4, followed by two-minute segments at the floor of zone 2. After warming up adequately, you should accelerate quickly to the midpoint of zone 4 and hold that rate for the remaining portion of the four-minute period.

At the end of four minutes, quickly decrease exercise intensity to the floor of zone 2 and stay at that level for the remainder of two minutes. Do five sets replicating four minutes at the midpoint of zone 4 and two minutes at the floor of zone 2. The total elapsed time is 38 minutes.

If you have a feature on your monitor called a "countdown timer," you should use it. It will give off an audible alarm every four minutes to signal when to change from the midpoint of zone 4 (85 percent) to the floor of zone 2 (60 percent) and then back up the heartbeat ladder again to the midpoint of zone 4.

As you improve and this workout becomes easier, increase the work interval (that's the zone 4 time) to five minutes of work and three minutes of active rest (zone 2). Or, if the workout is too difficult, adjust it by dropping down one entire heart zone.

Summary of Threshold Workout

Zone	Zone name	Time in zone	HZT points
5	Red line		
4	Threshold	20 min	80
3	Aerobic		
2	Temperate	8 min	16
1	Healthy Heart	10 min	10
Totals		**38 min**	**116**

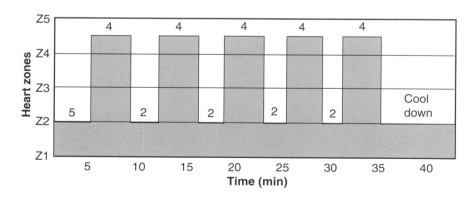

Outcome

With this workout, you want to try to improve your anaerobic threshold. This is an orange-zone workout, meaning it is designed for those with a higher fitness level. If you are training for a race or sport competition you may like the challenge of this workout. You can replace distance for time if you prefer to run by distance. You also can expand the duration progressively from 30 minutes to 36, 42, and 48 minutes. Be sure you have a recovery day—in the "Healthy Heart" or "Temperate" zone—following this workout.

From *Middle School Healthy Hearts in the Zone: A Heart Rate Monitoring Program for Lifelong Fitness* by Deve Swaim and Sally Edwards, 2002, Human Kinetics, Champaign, IL.

Workout V.10   Easy Does It

This is an interval workout in the low zones. The intensity ranges from 60 to 75 percent of Max HR. It is a simple series of two- and four-minute stages in zones 2 and 3. After warming up in zone 1, increase your heart rate to spend two minutes in zone 3 and then recover to the bottom of zone 2 (60 percent Max HR). As you get fitter, you may increase the work intervals by one minute, making the zone 3 period increase to three minutes, or four or more minutes, while simultaneously reducing recovery time to two minutes.

This workout can be done on any piece of aerobic equipment, but depending on the equipment, you may have to allow yourself more then five minutes for the buildup to the desired heart rate. Running or skating should be done on a track or other controlled surface to manage the pattern.

Summary of Easy Does It Workout

Zone	Zone name	Time in zone	HZT points
5	Redline		
4	Threshold		
3	Aerobic	12 min	36
2	Temperate	24 min	48
1	Healthy Heart	7 min	7
Totals		**43 min**	**91**

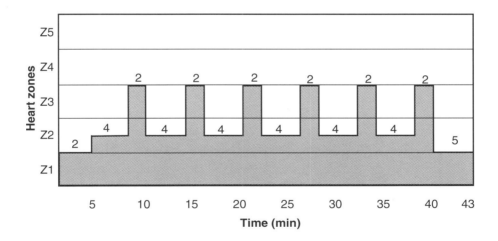

From *Middle School Healthy Hearts in the Zone: A Heart Rate Monitoring Program for Lifelong Fitness* by Deve Swaim and Sally Edwards, 2002, Human Kinetics, Champaign, IL.

Workout V.11   Twin Peaks

The purpose of this workout is to push your anaerobic threshold in order to achieve an improved level of fitness. This is a challenging workout and offers a multitude of benefits. It is also adaptable—you can substitute zone 2 and 3 intensities for the zones 3 and 4 shown here and achieve different cardiovascular benefits.

This 30-minute workout consists of two 15-minute periods. In each period, you gradually will increase the exercise effort. After seven minutes, you should be at or above the floor of your Threshold zone, 80 percent of Max HR. After you reach this peak heart rate number, of 80 percent Max HR, you should slow or back off your pace and recover to your Temperate zone 2 in seven to eight minutes. Next you start the climb again, seven minutes to the floor of your Threshold zone 4. Again you reduce your effort and recover to your zone 2. You continue your cool-down.

Summary of Twin Peaks Workout

Zone	Zone name	Time in zone	HZT points
5	Redline		
4	Threshold	10 min	40
3	Aerobic	20 min	60
2	Temperate	10 min	20
1	Healthy Heart	5 min	5
Totals		**45 min**	**125**

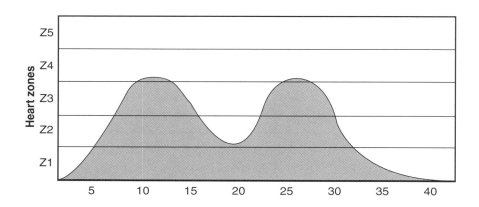

From *Middle School Healthy Hearts in the Zone: A Heart Rate Monitoring Program for Lifelong Fitness* by Deve Swaim and Sally Edwards, 2002, Human Kinetics, Champaign, IL.

APPENDIX A
HEART FACTS

The heart pushes more than 3 million quarts of blood a year through 60,000 miles of blood vessels in the human body.

At rest, the heart's output of blood is equivalent to 1,400 gallons a day, or about 37 million gallons over a 72-year lifetime.

The heart pumps six quarts of blood through more than 96,000 miles of blood vessels. This is the equivalent of 6,300 gallons being pumped per day. That is almost 115 million gallons in only 50 years.

The average heart weighs less than a pound yet pumps blood with incredible force. If you measured the power from your heart's 40 million beats per year, it would equal a force capable of lifting you 100 miles above the Earth.

APPENDIX B
TROUBLESHOOTING

If a heart rate monitor doesn't provide a readout or produces a series of misreads, try the following:

- Check the chest strap to make sure that it is snug. A loose chest belt acts like an intermittent electrical connection causing misreads.

- Make sure that the contact points are moist (there needs to be a certain amount of dampness for conductivity).

- Move the location of the transmitter to another location on the chest to see if it will have a flatter contact point. A person who has a concave chest can benefit from this tip. Transmitters work well when placed at the same height but on the back.

- Move away from airwaves' interference. Because the transmitter emits a fairly weak signal to the wrist monitor, other equipment can disturb the transmission. In a class situation always maintain a three-foot distance between each transmitter. Other interference may come from power lines or even airplanes, but these are usually short in duration and should not cause a problem.

- Make sure that the belt is snug enough. For students with very small chests, tie a flat knot in the belt elastic to shorten the chest strap. It should be snug but not inhibit movement or breathing.

APPENDIX C
BENEFITS OF AEROBIC EXERCISE

Improves bone calcium

Improves blood high-density cholesterol

Improves handling of excess heat

Increases hemoglobin

Improves resistance to cold

Decreases blood triglycerides

Gives an emotional lift

Decreases blood pressure

Decreases insulin requirement

Increases glycogen storage

Creates less conversion of sugar to fat

Increases stroke volume of heart

Decreases resting heart rate

Helps prevent senility—increases oxygen delivery to brain

Provides oxygen pickup in the lungs

Increases fat-burning enzymes

Helps fat deposits release fatty acids better

Allows better control of hunger

Decreases body fat

Decreases stress (attitude)

Increases ability to handle stress (biochemical)

Increases muscle mass

Makes it easier to exercise

Increases aerobic threshold

Makes possible a higher level of exercise

Burns more calories

Burns more fat calories

Causes more calories to be required at rest

Decreases load on the heart

Decreases muscle dependence on sugar

Decreases incidence of hypoglycemia

APPENDIX D
CHOOSING THE RIGHT HEART RATE MONITOR

Purchasing a heart rate monitor can be a lot like choosing a computer. When you first begin to shop, you may not know exactly which features you'll need. However, you don't want to limit yourself in the future just because you weren't originally familiar with some of the potential benefits. As with any other purchase, you need to consider three basic factors: What features do you need now? How might your needs grow? What is your budget?

Currently, there are about 50 different heart rate monitor models available and that number is growing. There are four categories of heart rate monitors:

- Class 1: The starter—a first timer's heart rate monitor

Basic heart rate monitors: heart rate only.

These heart rate monitors are the simplest to operate and least expensive to purchase. They are easy to recognize because they have no buttons to push. The only thing they do is display your heart rate in beats per minute. The numbers are big and easy to read and the "watches" are durable. They are ideal for beginners who are participating in any aerobic activity—swimming, walking, aerobics, cycling, and so forth. They currently range in price from $49 to $99.

- Class 2: Zone monitor for multipurpose beginning and intermediate exercise levels.

Intermediate heart monitors: one training zone/time of day/heart rate.

These monitors are very popular because they are a functional combination of sports wristwatch and heart monitor. They allow you to program in one training zone, display the time of day, and operate a stopwatch. Some models will calculate the heart rate recovery time. You can wear these heart monitors as sports wristwatches even when you aren't exercising. Prices begin at $79 and go up to $119.

- Class 3: Memory and manual downloadable monitors

Advanced heart monitors: stored data for later retrieval and review.

This type of monitor has several features and stores in its memory extensive information about your workout. This information may include average heart rate; lap times; and time spent in, above, or below your training zone. Many of the memory heart rate monitors have interval timers for countdowns and countups. These monitors are excellent for reviewing workouts and keeping track of progress over time. Prices range from $180 to $300.

- Class 4: Monitors for athletes, competitive training, maximum feedback

Competitive monitors: computer download for complete workout analysis.

These are the most sophisticated type of heart rate monitors and usually are called computer downloadable monitors. They are for the people who need precise training information for coaching or competition, and for those who want to store and analyze the information they receive. These monitors allow you to manually download data into a computer by either soniclink, infrared, or other types of transmission. Download monitors are priced from $199 to $369 and their accompanying download system and software is an additional $100 to $300.

Four Decisions for Buying or Upgrading Your Heart Rate Monitor

Decision 1. Of the four categories of monitors, which one has the features that are most important to you? Continuous-read monitors are the most user friendly. They are like the tachometer of your car. All you have to do is look at it and it only tells you one thing—your intensity number or how often your heart is beating in beats per minute.

If you think you may use your HRM as a training tool, a fitness management device, a stress-reduction instrument, or a fat control technology, you will need a monitor that gives you more data then a continuous-read one. However, it may take a week or so for you to learn to both program as well as understand all of the features. This is one of those times when you'll definitely want to read the manual.

If you are committed to training in less time but more intelligently, you may want to invest in a downloadable monitor. Purchasing a book on how to use the information will allow you to maximize the benefits it has to offer. It is up to you to decide how much of the information you wish to use. There is a lot of data available for you and interpreting it can be easier with a downloadable monitor.

Decision 2. Are maintenance and repair important to you? Some heart rate monitors allow you to change the batteries yourself. Others require sending it back to the manufacturer, which can take two to three weeks. All sports gear eventually suffers from wear and weather. Read the manufacturer's warranty before you make a decision.

Decision 3. What features do you want in a heart rate monitor? Do you want the additional features that a watch offers? How about the ability to program in your recovery time or time spent in multiple heart zones? Do you want a sampling of heart rate intervals? Keep in mind what your eventual goals are. Just because you do not need or understand some of these features now doesn't mean you won't need them. However, purchasing a classroom set of monitors that are easy to use at first is optimum.

Decision 4. Think about costs: how much bang do you want and how many bucks do you have? Sometimes people set budgets because they think that's how much they should spend on something; other times it's because that's all they can really afford. In 1983 heart rate monitors cost almost $500. Today they range the same as athletic shoes. Most of all, it is important to put a monitor on every student, so we generally recommend less features and more monitors.

APPENDIX E
HOW TO COMPLETE A LOG PAGE

Date: Record day and month.

Sport/activity: List the type of sport activity(ies) for the day.

Distance: Record the distance of each activity.

Time: Record the elapsed time of the activity.

Time in zone: Enter the number of minutes spent in each zone.

Workout benefit: List which of the three workout benefits this activity accomplishes: health, fitness, or performance.

Ambient HR: Record your ambient HR before you start the activity.

Rating: "Grade" the difficulty of this workout.

HZT points: To calculate points, multiply the heart zone number by the number of minutes spent in that heart zone. Example:

20 minutes in Zone 2 = 40 HZT points

15 minutes in Zone 3 = 45 HZT points

Total HZT points = 85

Weekly summary: Total for the week.

Year-to-date summary: Total for the year.

Notes: Reflect on the workout and put down ideas of what you would do differently next time.

Sample Completed Log Page

Date	Sport/ activity	Distance	Time	Z1	Z2	Z3	Z4	Z5	Workout benefit	Ambient HR	Rating	HZT points
				Time in zone								
3/15	Swim	1000	30 min	3 min	15 min	12 min	—	—	Fitness	62	B	69
3/16	Run	2 mi	30 min	—	10 min	2 min	—	—	Fitness			80
	Swim	1500	1:00	6 min	30 min	30 min	—	—	Performance	61	B	240
3/17	Rest day											
3/18	Bike	18 mi	1:15	—	9 min	41 min	25 min	6 min	Health	62	B+	271
3/19	Run	5 mi	45 min	10 min	12 min	28 min	—	—	Fitness	—	A	118
3/20	Bike	20 mi	1:15	—	15 min	60 min	—	—	Fitness	63	A	210
3/21	Run	6 mi	55 min	—	15 min	30 min	10 min	—	Performance	60	A	250
Weekly summary	Swim	2500	1:30	9 min	45 min	42 min	—	—				481
	Bike	38 mi	2:30	—	24 min	1:21	25 min	6 min		61.6	B+	309
	Run	13 mi	2:10	10 min	37 min	1:58	10 min	—				448
Year-to-date summary												

Notes: I am really enjoying this class. I'm getting fitter!

I want to make time to stretch more. I did stretch 5 x this week!

APPENDIX F
STUDENT HEART ZONE TRAINING LOG PAGE

This Heart Zone Training page belongs to: _____

Date	Sport/ activity	Distance	Time	Time in zone					Workout benefit	Ambient HR	Rating	HZT points
				Z1	Z2	Z3	Z4	Z5				
Weekly summary												
Year- to-date summary												
Notes:												

APPENDIX G
STUDENT JOURNAL PAGE

Date: _____

Lesson: _____

Questions to consider: What did I learn today? How will that impact my decisions/choices today, next week, next month, and next year?

_____

_____

_____

_____

_____

_____

_____

_____

_____

_____

_____

_____

_____

_____

_____

_____

_____

_____

_____

_____

_____

_____

From *Middle School Healthy Hearts in the Zone: A Heart Rate Monitoring Program for Lifelong Fitness* by Deve Swaim and Sally Edwards, 2002, Human Kinetics, Champaign, IL.

BIBLIOGRAPHY

American Medical Association Healthier Youth by the Year 2000 Project. 1991. *Healthy Youth 2000: National Health Promotion & Disease Prevention Objectives for Adolescents.* Chicago: American Medical Association.

Bar-Or, T., O. Bar-Or, H. Waters, A. Hirji, and S. Russell. 1996. Validity and social acceptability of the Polar Vantage XL for measuring heart rate in preschoolers. *Pediatr Exerc Sci* 8(2):115–121.

Best, R.W., and M.A. Steinhardt. 1991. The accuracy of children's counting of exercise heart rates. *Pediatr Exerc Sci* 3(3):229–237.

Bryant, D.M., A. Abraham, and M. Provost-Craig. 1996. Accuracy of self-reported heart rate at assessing exercise heart rate during aerobic dance. *Med Sci Sports Exerc,* Suppl, 28(5):209.

Carrol, T., R. Godsen, and C. Tangeman. 1991. The Polar Vantage XL heart rate monitor: An analysis of its internal consistency and computer interface. *Med Sci Sports Exerc,* Suppl, 23(4):14.

Durant, R.H., T. Baranowski, H. Davis, T. Rhodes, W.O. Thompson, K.A. Greaves, and J. Puhl. 1993. Reliability and variability of indicators of heart-rate monitoring in children. *Med Sci Sports Exerc* 25(3):389–395.

Edwards, Sally. 1994. *The Heart Rate Monitor Book.* Port Washington, N.Y.: Polar Electro.

———. 1996. *Heart Zone Training.* Holbrook, Mass.: Adams Media Corporation.

———. 1995. *The Heart Rate Monitor Log Book.* Sacramento, CA: Heart Zones Publishing.

———. 1997. *The Heart Rate Monitor Guidebook to Heart Zone Training.* Sacramento, CA: Heart Zones Publishing.

———. 2000. *The Heart Rate Monitor Book for Indoor and Outdoor Cyclists.* Boulder, CO: Velo Publishing.

———. 2001. *The Heart Rate Monitor Workbook.* Boulder, CO: Velo Publishing.

Godsen, R., T. Carroll, and S. Stone. 1991. How well does the Polar Vantage XL heart rate monitor estimate actual heart rate? *Med Sci Sports Exerc,* Suppl, 23(4):14.

Gretebeck, R.J., H.J. Montoye, D. Ballor, and A.P. Montoye. 1991. Comment on heart rate recording in field studies. *J Sport Med Phys Fit* 31(4):629–631.

Karvonen, J., J. Chwalbinska-Monet, and S. Säynäjäkangas. 1984. Validity and reliability of the heart rate monitors: Comparison of heart rates measured by ECG and microcomputer. *Physician and Sport Med* 12(6):65–69.

Katch, Frank, and William McArdle. 1996. *Exercise Physiology.* Philadelphia, PA: Lea and Febiger.

Laukkanen, R.M.T., and P. Virtanen. 1998. Heart rate monitors: State of the art. *J Sports Sci,* Suppl, July.

Leger, L., and M. Thivierge. 1988. Heart rate monitors: Validity, stability and functionality. *Physician and Sports Med* 16(5):143–151.

Lewis, D.J., and C. Salisury. 1992. An investigation into the accuracy of the Polar Favor and the Polar Edge heart rate monitors compared with direct ECG measurements. Report to Leisure System International. Officer Commanding Research & Training Flight, Royal Air Force School of Physical Training, Newcastle, U.K.

Loimaala, A., H. Sievänen, R. Laukkanen, J. Pärkkä, I. Vuori, and H. Huikuri. 1997. Accuracy of a real-time QRS detector for heart rate variability assessment. Abstract in *The XVIth Nordic Congress of Cardiology,* UKK Institute, Tampere, Finland.

Macfarlane, D.J., B.A. Fogarty, and W.C. Hopkins. 1989. The accuracy and variability of commercially available heart rate monitors. *The New Zealand Journal of Sports Medicine* 17(4):51–53.

Seaward, B.L., R.H. Sleamaker, T. McAuliffe, and J.F. Clapp. 1990. The precision and accuracy of a portable heart rate monitor. *Biomed Instrum Technol* 24(1):37–41.

Strand, B., and S. Reeder. 1993. PE with a heartbeat: Hi-tech physical education. *JOPERD* 64:81–84.

Thivierge, M., and L. Leger. 1988. Validity of heart rate monitors. *Sci et Sports* 3(3):211–221.

———. 1989. Critical review of heart rate monitors. *CAHPER J* 55(3):26–31.

Treiber, F.A., L. Musante, S. Hartdagan, H. Davis, M. Levy, and W.B. Strong. 1989. Validation of a heart rate monitor with children in laboratory and field settings. *Med Sci Sports Exerc* 21(3):338–342.

Trucano, Lucille. 1984. *Students Speak: A Survey of the Health Interests and Concerns of Over 5000 Washington State Students Kindergarten Through Twelfth Grade.* Seattle: CHEF.

U.S. Department of Health & Human Services. 1991. *Healthy People 2000: National Health Promotion & Disease Prevention Objectives.* U.S. Department of Health & Human Services, U.S. Government Office.

———. 1996. *Physical Activity and Health: A Report of the Surgeon General.* U.S. Department of Health & Human Services, Centers for Disease Control & Prevention, National Center for Chronic Disease Prevention and Health Promotion, The President's Council on Physical Fitness and Sport.

Vogelaere, P., F. De Meyer, W. Duquet, and P. Vandevelde. 1986. 'Sport Tester PE 3000' vs. Holter ECG for the measurement of heart frequency. *Belgique Sci et Sports* 1(4):321–329.

Wajciechowski, J.A., R.C. Gayle, R.L. Andrews, and G.B. Dintiman. 1991. The accuracy of radio telemetry heart rate monitoring during exercise. *Clinical Kinesiology* 45:9–12.

OTHER BOOKS ABOUT HEART ZONE TRAINING

Edwards, Sally. 1993. *The Heart Rate Monitor Book.* This is the best-selling book on how to use your heart rate monitor and it includes everything you need to know about how to maximize your cardiac-monitored exercise program.

———. 1994. *The Heart Rate Monitor Log.* Sacramento, CA: Heart Zones Publishing. If you use a heart rate monitor, it's key to record your workouts. The first of its kind, this log is designed exactly for keeping your heart rate data clearly and concisely. Here's a way to keep a diary of a year's worth of workouts in one book plus log your results from daily, weekly, and monthly events and activities.

———. 1996. *Heart Zone Training.* Learn how to get the most out of your workouts and your heart rate monitor regardless of your sport, level of fitness, or how much time you have to exercise. It's a breakthrough training program, easy to follow, and leads to immediate results.

———. 1998. *The Heart Rate Monitor Guidebook.* This is the leading-edge resource for anyone wanting to take that next step by learning more comprehensive information on heart rate-based monitoring and measurement. This book is recommended for all trainers, therapists, medical professionals, athletes, and weight-management professionals.

———. 2002. *School Curriculum Kit: The Complete Solution.* Sacramento, CA: Heart Zones Publishing. For the classroom teacher, this is the best way to implement your heart rate monitor based health and physical education program. It includes the heart rate monitor checkout station, a teacher's manual (for either middle school or high school), a copy of *The Heart Rate Monitor Book,* the maximum heart rate wall chart, 20 Heart Zone cards, and a 60 minute video. It comes packaged in a sturdy carrying case with the option to purchase a classroom set of monitors at discounted school prices.

Edwards, Sally and Sally Reed. 1999. *The Heart Rate Monitor Log.* Sacramento, CA: Heart Zones Publishing. This book contains a year's worth of log pages and information for you to record and evaluate your heart rate monitored workouts. Us this book as a training diary. It includes a glossary, training planner pages, and a buyer's guide to heart rate monitors.

———. 2000. *The Heart Rate Monitor Book for Outdoor and Indoor Cycling.* Boulder, CO: Velo Press. Edwards and Reed apply the already proven method of five-zone heart rate training to training for indoor/outdoor cyclists of all abilities. Included is a free CD-ROM that helps you ride your indoor or outdoor bike better.

———. 2000. *The Heart Rate Monitor Log for Cyclists.* Boulder, CO: Velo Press. Designed to complement the indoor and outdoor cyclists' workouts and rides, this log allows you to track your cycling goals and workout plans. Track a full year's worth of rides, every year!

———. 2001. *The Heart Rate Monitor Workbook.* Boulder, CO: Velo Press.

———. 2002. *The Heart Rate Monitor Guidebook to Heart Zone Training.* Sacramento, CA: Heart Zones Publishing. This book is written for the athletic enthusiast, the fitness professional, teachers, and those who want in-depth information about heart zone training. It is easy to read yet thorough on how to train using heart rate technology.

FOR MORE INFORMATION ABOUT HEART ZONE TRAINING

The Heart Zones Education creates and develops health and physical education curricula based on Heart Zone Training principles to monitor, assess, and manage wellness.

The Heart Rate Monitor Program for Health and Physical Education is a cardiac- or heart-based curriculum, which studies the heart and how it is affected by the mind, the emotions, physical activity, and diet. An advanced technological tool, the heart rate monitor, is used to give direct biofeedback about the response of the heart to these different stimuli and experiences.

The company offers a complete curriculum package, which includes a teaching manual, a checkout station, classroom sets of heart rate monitors, a heart zone wall chart, and a video.

In addition, the company provides training, consulting, seminars, and workshops to schools, organizations, and businesses. Further information is available upon request by contacting the following:

Deve Swaim, President
Heart Zones Education
P.O. Box 962
Canby, OR 97013
E-mail: HeartZTEd@aol.com

Heart Zones Education
2636 Fulton Ave. #100
Sacramento, CA 95821

To place an order:
Web site: www.heartzone.com
Heart Zones office phone: 916-481-7283
Heart Zones office fax: 916-481-2213

INDEX

Note: The italicized *f* and *t* following page numbers refer to figures and tables, respectively.

ABOUT THE AUTHORS

Deve Swaim, MS, is president of Heart Zones Education. For the past 25 years, she has been a health education advocate, teacher, and innovator. Her teaching and training experience extends from middle schools through the university level with expertise in curriculum development. She has won numerous educational awards and has served at the executive level for many professional organizations such as the Northwest District for the American Alliance for Health, Physical Education, Recreation and Dance and the Oregon Governor's Council on Physical Fitness and Sports. She has shared her knowledge at numerous programs and conventions across the country and internationally. Swaim is past executive director of the Oregon Health Promotion Foundation and represented Oregon on the National Coalition of Health Promotion Foundations. She currently teaches in the Graduate Teacher Education Program at Portland State University in Portland, Oregon.

Swaim is an avid fitness and movement enthusiast, a mother, an artist, and a lifetime resident of Oregon. As she comments, "Teaching middle school students health education has been one of my professional high points, because when kids learn their enthusiasm is contagious and exciting." Other health professionals say about Swaim that her energy and enthusiasm for health education is more than contagious—it shows a true commitment to making a difference with a vision.

Since 1997, Swaim has dedicated herself to creating and developing the Heart Zones Education and writing the first curriculum applications. During that time she directed all phases of building and shaping the material, testing it in the school setting, inputting the revisions, and upgrading its strategies and application. The company's first product line, the Heart Rate Monitor Program for Middle School Health and Physical Education, is being taught by award-winning teachers across the country.

Sally Edwards, MA, MBA, is the head heart of Heart Zones Education. A world-class athlete and best-selling author, Edwards is considered one of America's leading authorities on health, fitness, and sports. She literally wrote the book on heart rate-based fitness with her six titles: *Heart Zone Training, The Heart Rate Monitor Book, The Heart Rate Monitor Guidebook to Heart Zone Training,* and three books on bicycling with a heart rate monitor. In addition to winning races from a mile to a hundred miles, she holds a lifetime secondary teaching license in physical education. Edwards has started more than a half dozen successful businesses. She enjoys balancing a fitness lifestyle with racing in some of the hardest races in the world, including Race Across America, adventure races such as Eco Challenge, and the 16 Ironman triathlon finishes. She is a member of the Triathlon Hall of Fame.

Edwards designed the Heart Zone Training program and has served as a cowriter and developer of Heart Zone Education curricula.